M000206100

CRASH–TEST INVESTING

How to Put Seat Belts on Your Portfolio for the Bumpy Road Ahead

BRAD McMILLAN

Copyright © 2018 by William Bradford McMillan, Jr.

All rights reserved.

No part of this publication may be reproduced, stored in a retrieval system, or transmitted in any form or by any means, electronic, mechanical, photocopying, recording, scanning, or otherwise, except as permitted under Section 107 or 108 of the 1976 United States Copyright Act, without the prior written permission of the author.

Limit of Liability/Disclaimer of Warranty: While the publisher and the author have used their best efforts in preparing this book, they make no warranties with respect to the accuracy or completeness of the contents of the book and specifically disclaim any implied warranties or merchantability or fitness for a particular purpose. No warranty may be created or extended by sales representatives or written sales materials. The advice and strategies contained herein may not be suitable for your situation. You should consult with a professional where appropriate. Neither the publisher nor the author shall be liable for any loss of profit or any other commercial damages, including, but not limited to special, incidental, consequential, or other damages.

To my wife, Nora, and son, Jackson

CONTENTS

FOREWORD

As a passionate fan of professional sports, I both follow my favorite teams as well as watch and study the business of sports. One of the most intriguing elements on the management side of things is the draft—the annual process of selecting new players to add to existing teams. This often incites debate among fans, media, and other "experts" about each team's most critical need and which player can best meet that need. Another school of thought focuses solely on selecting the best athlete available, regardless of need.

As CEO of Commonwealth Financial Network, I understand the problem—and the challenge. I work with nearly 1,800 financial advisors across the country, and I hear firsthand what they need to help their clients pursue their goals. My job is to put together the best team to deliver on those needs. It's not always easy. Sometimes, though, the answer is crystal clear: if market and economic analysis were a sport, and I had the first pick in the draft, my selection of Brad McMillan would be a slam dunk.

I have worked with Brad, who is chief investment officer at Commonwealth, for almost 12 years. I remember interviewing him back in November 2006. A smart and articulate man, he showed up at our door with an alphabet of credentials on his résumé. It was obvious he was the right person for the job, and yet we've all seen first-round draft picks flame out. Time would tell if I made the right choice in hiring Brad—and time has shown that my all-star pick had an incredible upside that I didn't see coming!

Though his intellect was never in question, it's Brad's analysis and communication style that has set him apart. It has proven to be both accurate and timely, plus it's delivered in a manner that's easy to understand and apply. Brad is a storyteller who explains difficult concepts in relatable terms. He also brings a command of human behavior and common sense to his commentary that makes his message enjoyable as well as practical.

Brad's themes are evergreen, but the timing for *Crash-Test Investing* couldn't be better. After an unprecedented decade-long equity market run-up, and with interest rates now on the rise, it's important to step back and assess the risk in your portfolio and consider strategies that will help insulate against the volatility that's sure to come.

Whether you manage your own money, or you work with a professional advisor, this book will help you make better investment decisions that hopefully produce even more meaningful outcomes.

Wayne Bloom, CEO
Commonwealth Financial Network

WHY YOU SHOULD
READ THIS BOOK

There are many excellent books on investing. Most of them, however, assume you have lots of interest in and time to spend on managing your money. Most people don't.

In that way, investing is like driving a car. For some people, it is fun and exciting, even a bit dangerous, but for most people, it's simply a way to get where you want to go as quickly and safely as possible.

Unfortunately, with investing, just as with driving a car, sometimes you get into trouble. When the weather gets bad, when other drivers act irresponsibly, whatever it might be, crashes happen. That's when you are very glad to be wearing your seat belt.

This book offers a way to invest with seat belts, which can help you survive a market crash with minimum damage. Cars come with seat belts, but investing has been different. The standard belief is that occasional crashes are unpredictable and unavoidable, and people simply must accept that and ride them out.

Historically—from, say, 1950 through 2000—it was possible to do just that. Many people saved, retired, and did well. It made sense to sit tight and ride out any downturns. Indeed, the argument that what has worked in the past will work in the future is a powerful one.

I contend, however, that conditions have changed. With two crashes in the past 20 years—and with market conditions now (in mid-2018) disturbingly like they were prior to those earlier crashes—we're dealing with a different reality.

Strategies that have worked in the past may not work in the future. Expectations that people have had in the past may not be met. Betting that everything will be the same in the next 20 years as it has been in the past 20 is no longer a reliable proposition.

This book will show you how to invest successfully while significantly lowering your risk of serious loss—even in a crash—without making it a full-time job.

WHAT YOU
NEED TO KNOW

You need to invest

The reality is you need to invest, almost regardless of how you choose to do so. By simply putting your money in the bank, not only do you risk failure, but you *guarantee* it.

Investing is inherently risky (though some risks *are* avoidable), and the biggest risk of all is inflation. Every year, the dollar is worth less, a trend that has continued for decades and shows no sign of slowing. In effect, every dollar you save is losing value every second it sits in the bank.

Inflation is low as I write this, but there are signs that it is increasing. Rent, food, and health care, for example, cost more every year. Over time, inflation can slowly erode your portfolio, like waves against a coastline.

You need to invest just to stay even with the loss in purchasing power due to inflation. To get ahead, you need to invest more aggressively. As we will discuss, stocks are the only asset class that, over time, allow you to make meaningful, real gains in purchasing power. Saving is not enough—you need to invest.

You need to invest in stocks

You hear a lot about the risks involved in the stock market, and those risks are real. At the same time, the stock market *should* go up over time. A rising stock market is a consequence of a growing, wealthier nation, and investing is a way to benefit from that.

Although we have our challenges and issues, the U.S. is uniquely well positioned in the world to do well over the next couple of decades. The energy boom alone should ensure a growing economy, but we also have a rising demographic boost from the echo boomers (i.e., the millennials) that should materialize in the next decade, a growing manufacturing recovery, and a highly skilled workforce.

We also benefit geographically, in that our neighbors to the north and south pose no threat, and oceans to the east and west provide some protection as well. In fact, I could write a book (and maybe I will) that covers many of the reasons why the U.S. should do well. Regardless, the data suggests that the future looks bright.

Combined, these factors have helped position the U.S. economy to grow at least as fast as, and probably faster than, any other country in the world over the next 20 years or so. A growing economy should help ensure a growing stock market over that same period. To participate in that growth, you need to invest in stocks.

You need to diversify—and more

Even though you must own stocks if you want to build wealth over time, stocks are not always a good place to be. Financial theory recommends that you diversify your investments—that is, put your money in other places besides stocks. The theory is that if stocks go down, other assets—usually bonds—will go up. This works, by and large, but in a crash, all financial assets often go down together.

Diversification addresses the risk associated with specific investments, but it does not address risk in the system itself. We saw a good example of this type of risk in 2008, when the whole system almost collapsed—taking all assets down with it. In that environment, the only real way to have preserved capital was to have been out of the market entirely. What happened in 2008 was a real crash test for portfolios, and many of them failed.

That failure of prevailing financial theory to cope with the risks inherent in a true market crash is what drove me to write this book. I saw too many people suffer. Diversification *does* help reduce risk, but it is not bulletproof. You need a way to protect yourself from risks to the whole system as well.

How we will get there

You will hear two themes repeatedly throughout this book: Main Street and seat belts. Main Street refers to strategies designed to be implemented simply and easily, designed for people who have lives that don't revolve around investing. Seat belts are strategies designed to help you walk away from a market crash with as little damage to your portfolio as possible.

Building a portfolio with seat belts, in a Main Street way, meets the goals of most investors. This book will show you a very effective way to accomplish that.

INVESTING
IS A JOURNEY

I have spent years working on a way to describe investing in a Main Street way, and the closest I have come is to compare it to a summer driving trip. When I was younger, flying was not an option; it was too expensive. Instead, we loaded up the car and drove to our destination.

Looking back, I marvel at my parents' commitment to taking my sister and me on those trips (and not abandoning me at some rest stop). Even more, I marvel at the risks we took. Back in the day, seat belts were optional. Kids ran amok in the back seat. Airbags were unheard of. Drinking and driving, if not necessarily accepted, was fairly common. It's a miracle anyone survived.

Today, of course, things are different. Kids are strapped into car seats. Drivers and passengers are protected by airbags. Drivers are, at least in theory, stone-cold sober when they get behind the wheel. And, in fact, these safety standards have worked: traffic fatalities are down significantly since the 1960s. The roads are safer, and the chance of surviving your journey is much, much higher.

Contrast this with investing. Not only do we not have the equivalent of airbags and seat belts, but their existence is actively denied. Standard investment wisdom says explicitly that return is dependent on risk. If you want to reach your goals—not just quickly, but at all—you must deal with the occasional crash, so hold on tight!

Worse than that, the chance of a crash—a big, life-threatening one—has increased. Looking at the chart below, we can see that two of the largest crashes in history have taken place in the past 20 years.

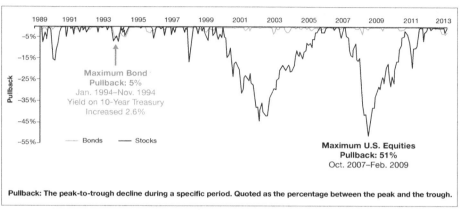

Source: http://blog.helpingadvisors.com/2013/11/07/bond-bashing-like-its-1999/

Morningstar monthly maximum drawdown percentage for the Bloomberg Barclays U.S. Aggregate Bond Index (Bonds) and the Russell 3000® Index (Stocks) from December 31, 1989, to September 30, 2013. Indices are unmanaged, and investors cannot invest directly in an index. Index returns represent past performance, are not a guarantee of future performance, and are not indicative of any specific investment.

The risks on the road

In the past 35 years, we have had only three significant market declines: in 1987, 2000, and 2008. The two biggest have occurred in the past 20 years. Big stock market drops seem to be coming more frequently. What's going on?

People will tell you that it is impossible to determine when the market is in risky territory. I am naturally suspicious of statements like this; I want to see real data. As it happens, we *do* have data that allows us to see when risk is high.

Let's use our car analogy. What gets people in trouble when driving? Usually, they drive too fast for conditions, get distracted, or both. The same can be said of the stock market.

Stocks should grow with the economy as a whole. Sometimes, though, they grow much faster—going too fast for conditions. At the same time, investors lose sight of this simple fact and get distracted—by, for example, the idea of a New Economy (in 1999) or the notion that housing prices will continue to increase (in 2007). This can go on for years, as we saw, but in each case, a crash became more and more likely.

When you drive fast, or when stocks are expensive, a damaging crash is more likely. This is common sense. The faster you go, or the more expensive the market, the worse the crash is likely to be.

As investors evaluating our journey, we need to understand how risky the road is right now. How much crash risk is there? One of the best ways to figure this out is to look at how expensive the stock market is.

The best way to measure this is by examining how much a stock is selling for relative to its earnings. Paying $10 for $1 of earnings yields better results, over time, than paying three times the price, or $30, for the same $1 of earnings. "Buy cheap" is the first rule of market success, and this is really the way the market works, as stock prices are often expressed as *price-to-earnings*, or *P/E*, ratios.

You can think of the P/E ratio as the price of the stock market, and you can calculate how much you would have made, over time, when the market was at various price levels.

To do this, let's look at the S&P 500, one of the major stock market indices in the U.S. It measures 500 of the largest companies in the country, so it is a good representation of the entire stock market. I calculated how expensive the index was each month from 1970 to 2009, and then I calculated how much an investment in the index would have made over the next five and ten years. Using common sense, you would expect results starting from when the market was cheap to be better than results starting from when it was expensive, and the table shows this to be true. We will discuss this in more depth later, but for now, note that buying when the market is cheap typically results in higher returns than buying when the market is expensive.

Average Returns by Starting Valuation		
P/E	Average returns, next 10 years	Average returns, next 5 years
35–45; most expensive	0.02%	−1.55%
25–34.99; we are here	*7.51%*	*4.92%*
15–24.99	11.54%	12.96%
5–14.99; least expensive	15.23%	14.60%

Source: Brad McMillan's personal research

Why do expensive markets result in subpar returns? The answer is that high prices usually adjust downward, often substantially. In other words, when markets get going too fast, they tend to crash. Let's look at a chart of longer-term P/E ratios and see what happened when they reached high levels.

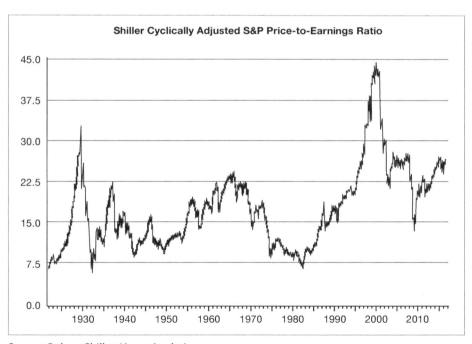

Source: Robert Shiller, Haver Analytics

The previous chart looks back to the 1920s, and there are a couple of points worth noting. First, the peaks in valuations occurred in 1929, the late 1960s, 1973–1974, 1987, 2000, 2008, and right around mid-2017. Some of these dates might ring a bell, particularly 1929, 1987, 2000, and 2008. Every single peak except the one in mid-2017 was followed by a significant decline in stock prices—and the jury is still out on the latter.

When you pay a high price for a stock—or a house, as many did in the mid-2000s—you may be lucky enough to find someone to pay more later, but the higher the price you pay, the tougher it will be.

Borrowing too much can get people, and markets, in trouble as well. We saw this during the housing bubble in the mid-2000s, when buyers took out huge loans, confident that prices would keep going up. The same thing happens in the stock market.

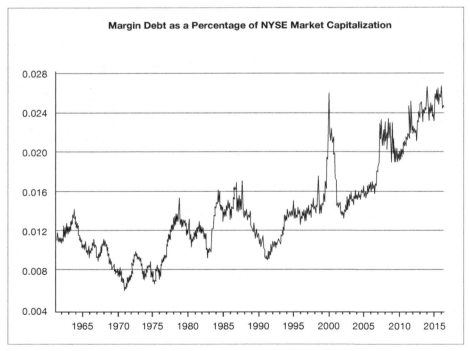

Source: Haver Analytics

One way to assess how much debt is in the stock market is to divide the debt by the total value of all stocks in the market, which is what the previous chart shows. Although we're not looking at the same period as in the P/E chart, we can see some of the same peaks. Look at 1987, for example, or 2000, or 2008. In each past case, a spike in debt led to a substantial decline in the market. As I write this, we're approaching similarly high levels.

I am not saying that a crash is coming tomorrow. Valuations can remain high for years, and both economic and earnings growth could potentially normalize the market without a significant decline. Risk levels have clearly increased, however. With valuations where they are, and with lots of debt in the system, it looks quite a bit like it did in 1999 and 2007. The market is driving pretty fast on an increasingly slippery road.

Planning the trip

Thinking of investing as a journey makes sense to me. You set out with a map and a plan for getting to your final destination. Along the way, you might encounter bad weather, construction zones, careless drivers, whining kids, the need to get gas or stop to use the restroom—you get the idea.

The point I'm trying to make is that the goal, your destination, is more important than the journey in most cases. All you really want is to arrive healthy and safe. This is the Main Street approach to investing: to reach your goals—retirement, college, or whatever—with enough money to achieve them. It is clear that market conditions are risky as I write this, so anyone investing today should want a way to minimize the chance of serious loss. Driving conditions look a bit scary, so it is definitely time to think about putting on your seat belt.

In this book, we will consider several different strategies for helping you reach your goals, looking at the costs and benefits of each. We will examine the ways these strategies can succeed, as well as how they might fail. We will also compare them with other methods for getting to the same destination.

Investing is and will continue to be the best way for the average person to meet his or her financial goals. My objective is to give you some simple rules and tactics to help you arrive at your destination quickly and safely, with the minimum necessary costs and risks.

WHERE DO YOU WANT TO GO?

Let's talk about your financial journey. Many investment books focus on making as much money as possible as quickly as possible. In the real world, financial goals are a bit more complicated. Not that we don't want to make money; quite the contrary! For most of us, though, this is not our sole focus. Most of us have families and lives, and money is a means to an end rather than an end in itself.

This difference in focus—reaching goals versus making money—is what drives the seat belt approach we are using here. Rather than trying to go as fast as possible, we want to get to our destination safely. Occasional crashes are an inevitable part of the journey, but we want to drive responsibly, if as fast as reasonable.

The importance of timing

Most people's goals are pretty simple. The most common are buying a house, paying for college, and retiring comfortably. For every one of these goals, piling up as much money as possible is important, but it is not the only factor.

Equally as important is *timing*. When you want to buy a house, the long-term view doesn't matter that much. You want to move in soon. When your kid turns 18, the idea of waiting 10 years for the market to recover so you can pay for college is tough to stomach. Likewise, at 65, the notion of postponing retirement loses much of its appeal. For most people, financial needs are very time dependent.

Financial theory considers risk in the context of maximizing returns and the variability of the returns that you will experience on that journey. In many respects, it resembles an auto race more than a drive to the corner store. This is great in a Wall Street context, but for someone who lives on Main Street, the goal is to get to the destination on time, with a minimum of danger. Both views are valid, but the latter is more appropriate for someone who wants to buy a house, send his or her kids to college, or retire.

Imagine you bought an investment for your retirement that does incredibly well, making you tons of money. Then, it collapses when you turn 65. Does this do you any good? Now compare it to an investment that does not do as well but never collapses. You may make less money at the peak, but you have a better chance of keeping and spending it.

This chapter will discuss the advantages and disadvantages of both types of investing. We all struggle with the notion of making money versus taking risk. To properly understand what we really want and need to do, we need to take a hard look at what specifically constitutes success—and, just as important, failure—in our chosen journey. More, we need to do that over the context of our entire journey, not just the first couple of years.

Main Street investing is about planning that journey and getting you there safely. So, let's look at the map for a couple of the most common destinations: college and retirement.

College planning

College planning has two defining aspects: a limited time period—in most cases, less than 20 years—and a more or less definite start and end date. Unlike retirement, there is less flexibility in the start point but much less uncertainty as to the duration of the expense. Sure, some people may not be able to hit the start-at-18 and finish-at-22 goalposts, but these markers define what many people expect when they engage in college planning.

How do we measure success, and what would failure look like? This is difficult in that we generally don't know which school a child will attend or how much it will cost. Ideally, we would have enough to fully fund a Harvard education, so let's aim to end up with as much money as we can while minimizing the chance that our strategy will blow up at the wrong time—just before writing that first tuition check.

Let's consider first what returns we need to realize in order to meet our goals and then move on to the different ways to make sure we get those returns. After that, we'll consider some of the risks we face and the different ways we might fail.

We know that higher education costs have increased at an average rate of around 6 percent per year. Just to keep pace, we need returns of at least 6 percent, and ideally, we would show real growth above that level.

That return has to come over an (assumed) 10-year time horizon, since little Johnny/Amanda is 8 years old right now. These are the questions we must answer:

1. How do we evaluate the level of returns we can expect?

2. What risks should we be looking at?

3. How can we tell the amount of risk we face?

These questions are at the heart of this book. We will deal with them in detail later on, but the quick answers are as follows:

1. The one determining factor for future returns is how expensive the stock market is when you begin investing. We can come up with a pretty good estimate based on history, although relying on past performance does have its flaws.

2. By defining our goal so specifically, we can determine that there are two risks. First, we might not have enough money; this is the *return risk*. Second, we might end up with enough money, only to have the market crash and eliminate our gains just before or during college; this is *drawdown risk*. With a smaller and already known shortfall, return risk can be mitigated by borrowing, saving more, or adjusting expectations. Drawdown risk, which is often sudden and unexpected, would be much harder to mitigate.

3. Given that sudden risk is the biggest concern, we can evaluate our risks against the likelihood of a sudden decline. Again, history can provide us with a guide as well as some conditions that indicate when it's time to worry.

An example. Let's use my son, Jackson, as an example. He is now 10, and I hope he will go to college when he is 18 and graduate in four years. I have about eight years to save.

College now costs, on average, around $25,000 per year, or $100,000 for four years. With higher education costs growing at around 6 percent per year, if I had $100,000 right now to invest, I could pay for my son's education if I earned that same return on my investments, setting aside any taxes I pay.

In theory, I could put all the money in stocks. Over the past 10 years, the S&P 500 (the index of the share prices of 500 large U.S. companies and a standard benchmark for the stock market) has returned more than 8 percent, on average. Over the past 20 years, it has returned more than 9 percent, which would easily cover the rising costs.

The problem is that twice during the past 18 years, in 2000 and 2008–2009, the market proceeded to lose a substantial amount of value. Had Jackson been going to college in 2001 or 2010, I would not have had the money to pay his tuition.

Return potential also varies depending on the price you pay when you first invest in stocks. When the market is expensive, returns are likely to be lower, whereas they are likely to be higher when it is cheap. So, if you buy when the market is expensive, your expected returns may well be below that 8 percent–9 percent we talked about.

This highlights the return risk we face. In addition, higher valuations also mean a higher drawdown risk. An expensive market not only means you can expect to make less, but it also means you stand to lose more in the event of a crash. You, therefore, must consider all these factors when determining how much to invest and when. If you are lucky enough to set aside enough to pay for college, of course, the point is moot, and you can stay in cash with no risk at all. For most people, though, that option is unavailable.

The nice thing about college planning is that it covers a relatively short time, both in saving and in spending; therefore, any errors may be solved by borrowing, scholarships, a work-study program, or some other means. Retirement planning is not nearly as simple.

Retirement planning

Retirement planning is harder than college planning. First, it covers a longer saving period. Second, the timing of retirement is much less certain, and this flexibility provides both options and uncertainty. Third, the spending period is much longer, generally decades rather than four years, which introduces multiple other risks.

The goal, though, remains the same: save as much as possible, grow it as much as you can, and try to avoid having it blow up either before or during your retirement. The stakes are much higher in this case, of course. Because you will no longer be working, taking out a loan and paying it back will be difficult. Nor are there scholarships to help fund your retirement. By the time you know you've failed, it may be too late.

Again, we need to consider what returns we need to realize in order to meet our goals and understand the different ways to ensure that we get those returns. And, of course, we need to understand the risks we face and the different ways we might fail.

History can be our guide. This time, however, we must consider longer periods of time. Differences in returns over longer compounding periods can result in significantly different final values. For most of the saving period, therefore, returns are more important than interim drawdowns, and we should prioritize them. As we approach the retirement period, though, *drawdown risk*—the risk of losing money in a sudden market decline—becomes paramount, which brings us to the second question: what risks should we be looking at? Here, the risks are lower-than-expected returns during the saving period and drawdown risks both as we approach the retirement period and after we retire.

The longer time frame also affects how we evaluate our risks. For returns, hitting at least the target return is the primary risk. Again, excess returns are nice, but below-target returns mean failure. Drawdowns, insofar as they drop returns below target, remain a significant concern as well, even in this scenario.

An example. Retirement planning has all the same risks as college planning, with the additional wrinkle that, after you retire, you likely will begin withdrawing and spending your money. We know college costs are rising at about 6 percent per year. Your cost of living in retirement probably will increase at or slightly above the inflation rate, say 3 percent. But you will also need to withdraw some amount—the current rule of thumb is 4 percent—to cover living expenses. You, therefore, need to make at least 7 percent to meet expenses without spending down your capital.

Most people intend to spend down their capital over time, so, in effect, a lower return still works, but this gives rise to *longevity risk*, or the risk of outliving your income. The higher the return, the less chance you will run out of money when you can least afford to.

What happens, though, if your investments lose a big chunk of their value due to a decline in the market (i.e., a drawdown)? Unlike during the saving cycle, you are not putting money in to replace the loss; in fact, you are pulling money out, compounding the effect of the drawdown. Further, when your balance declines, you either must reduce your income or accept the fact that the withdrawals will become an even bigger percentage of your portfolio.

For example, assume you have a $100,000 portfolio. You plan on pulling $4,000 (4 percent) out the first year, then increasing that by 3 percent each year to offset increasing prices. You need a return of about 7 percent per year to do both, or about $7,000 ($4,000 for spending and $3,000 to counter the effects of inflation).

Suppose the market drops 25 percent. You now have a $75,000 portfolio, and the $7,000 in spending and inflation growth you counted on is now 9 percent of your balance instead of 7 percent. You either must take less, now and forever, or start getting higher returns. This risk is worse early in retirement, but it continues for as long as you live.

Wall Street, in the form of conventional financial theory, would say, in both cases, that the market will recover in the long run. Main Street says we may not be around in the long run, and, in any event, we need the money *now*. We need to deal with these risks.

The sleep-at-night factor

There's another factor that is not reflected in conventional financial models; it's what I call the sleep-at-night factor. How much can you lose from your investments and still be able to sleep at night?

One way to determine this is to fill out a risk assessment questionnaire. In theory, you answer the questions, and you get an idea of how much risk you are comfortable with. The problem with this approach has to do with the precise definition of risk being used, which, as we know, may be different than how you really *think* of risk.

People deal with risk in the abstract very differently than they do in reality. How questions are asked can make a big difference in the results. For example, asking someone if they could tolerate losing 20 percent is one thing. But asking whether they could tolerate losing $20,000 on a $100,000 portfolio both sounds and is very different.

Sticking with a strategy during a drawdown can be hard. Many people abandoned the market in 2009, just before the recovery. In doing so, they locked in losses instead of participating in gains.

What we are trying to do here is design portfolios that minimize loss and then test them in various crashes over history to see whether our design would have worked. If you knew that a portfolio design had never lost more than 15 percent, while generating a return of 8 percent, over the past 30 years, you might have more confidence in the future.

By understanding what we are doing, why we are doing it, and what risks we are taking—and how those risks have played out in the past—we can design a system that allows us to reach our goals while sleeping better at night.

A LESSON IN RISK

There are two pieces to investing: *risk* and *return*. Most people think about returns in terms of how much money they can make. That makes sense, as everyone wants to make money—and at the end of the day, that is what investing is all about. Returns are only half the picture, though, and they're the less important half at that. The more important half is risk. I don't care how much I can win at Russian roulette; I'm not going to play.

What do we mean when we talk about risk? When most people think of risk, they worry about losing money. Money at risk, in my mind, is money I can lose.

The wrong way to measure risk

This is not how risk is treated in financial theory, though. In financial theory, risk is defined as how much returns bounce around. A stock, or fund, that loses the same amount of money every period would be viewed as a low-risk investment, simply because you know how it would perform. You might not invest in it, of course, but it still would be low risk.

Similarly, the riskiness of a portfolio would be viewed as how much the return fluctuates—not whether it makes money, or how much it loses at any one time.

Mathematically, you can make an argument for looking at risk this way. The units of measure used—the mean return and the standard deviation—show how much the expected return should be and how much it might vary above and below that amount. What this analysis fails to capture, however, is the likelihood of a crash that would derail your financial plans. So, from the perspective of a typical investor, it does not really solve the problem.

Risk in the real world

With financial theory and standard investment practice treating risk in this way, the question we should ask is whether such an approach really works. History suggests that it fails at the worst times.

Let's look at the most recent crisis, in 2008. One way to diversify your holdings was (and still is) to split investments between stocks and bonds. In fact, a portfolio of 60-percent stocks and 40-percent bonds is considered industry shorthand for a balanced, diversified portfolio.

With this kind of portfolio, however, significant loss is a very real possibility in the event of a crash. During the 2008 financial crisis, stock prices dropped by more than half. That industry standard portfolio, with 60-percent stocks and 40-percent bonds, would have dropped by almost one-third. Think about being a new retiree planning to live off that money and seeing one-third of it vanish. No matter how well the market does subsequently, that loss can scar. Was this risk captured in the standard statistics? It was not.

The typical investment manager argument is that the risk of substantial loss is an inevitable consequence of the ability to make money over time. There are several problems with this argument:

1. It's simply incorrect. Many studies have shown that, over time, less volatile and risky stocks have generated higher returns.

2. There are several simple methodologies that have been very successful in generating competitive returns with lower risk, measured in the commonsense way (i.e., by how much money you might lose at any one time).

3. Even if it were true (it's not), for the investor who needs the money soon, that much risk is unacceptable.

There is a better way, and I will show you.

HOW INVESTORS FAIL

If we are going to take the wheel in our investing journey, we must understand how the car works—how to steer, where the brakes and accelerator are. This is not optional if we want to get to our destination.

Most important, we need to understand the risks because if we can minimize our risks, we are more than halfway to success. You've heard about much of what we will cover here in previous sections. Now, we will take a different perspective, one oriented toward determining what we can expect to happen, and why, and what that means for our ultimate goals.

Failure risk: Slow and fast

The first thing we need to understand is risk. In our case, what we mean by risk is the chance that we will not meet our investing goals in the long term. By stating it this way, we can cut out things that might seem important, but ultimately are not, and keep our eyes on the final destination.

To understand risk, you must understand how you might fail in your objectives. Ernest Hemingway wrote in *The Sun Also Rises*:

"How did you go bankrupt?" Bill asked.

"Two ways," Mike said. "Gradually and then suddenly."

Slow failure: Return risk. The first way to fail in your investing journey is simply by not having enough return to meet your financial goals over time. This is slow failure. It is subtle and can be hard to spot, but inflation is a good example.

When inflation rises faster than your portfolio, you are effectively losing purchasing power every year, even when you think you are making money. Prices go up every year, and if your investments go up by less, then you can buy less with that money. We address slow failure by making sure we understand our required return level and constructing a portfolio that can effectively generate the returns we need.

Fast failure: Drawdown risk. The second risk is when the market drops and you lose money when you can least afford to do so. In the college planning example, this would be just as your student is prepared to leave for freshman year. In the retirement planning scenario, this could be any number of years before or after your target retirement date. If you lose that money, you may not be able to meet your withdrawal goals and still have a reasonable probability of having your money last as long as you do. This is fast failure.

- So, return risk is slow failure. We must drive fast enough to get to our destination on time—that is, we must invest in a way that will generate returns high enough to allow us to meet our realistic goals.
- Drawdown risk, or portfolio crash risk, is fast failure. Even if we have a car that will go fast enough, or a portfolio that will earn enough money, we still might crash. We do not want a portfolio to blow up on us just before we get to our destination, even if we have made good time getting there.

The problem we have as Main Street investors is, therefore, twofold: How do we construct a portfolio to go fast enough to get us the returns we need? And how do we simultaneously manage that portfolio to avoid crashing it? *Is* there a way to protect our portfolios from those losses? Can we put seat belts on our investments?

We can. There are costs, of course—nothing is free—but there are simple strategies that can meaningfully limit your exposure in the event of a crash while still generating the returns you need to reach your goals.

Why controlling risk is so important
One of the things you need to understand about risk is that losses hurt more than gains feel good. This is a fact in two ways. First, there's the psychology of it.

Studies have shown that losing a certain amount of money hurts a heck of a lot more than the pleasure we feel at gaining the same amount of money. For our own mental health, we, therefore, must try to limit losses—because the more you lose, the harder it will be for you to make rational decisions.

Although our innate reaction to loss appears emotional on the surface, it turns out to be quite rational because when you look at the risk, you see that losses hurt more mathematically than gains as well.

We can illustrate this with a pretty simple example. Say you start with $100. Now, assume you lose half of that, or 50 percent, so you have $50 remaining. Now that you've lost 50 percent, how much do you have to gain to get back to $100?

Even though you lost 50 percent, you must gain 100 percent—or $50 on the $50 you have left—to get back to where you started. Think about that: a 50-percent loss has to be followed by a 100-percent gain just to break even.

The math continues to work with smaller losses. If you lose one-third of your money, or 33 percent, for example, you need a 50-percent return to break even. If you lose one-quarter of your money, or 25 percent, you must get a 33-percent return to break even. The numbers start to match more closely with smaller losses, evening out around 10 percent; for example, if you have a 10-percent loss, you need an 11-percent gain to break even. You will always need to gain more than you lost to break even, however.

Why are we going through this? In order to succeed as investors in the long term, both psychologically and financially, we must balance our losses and our gains. Because losses and gains balance out around 10 percent, if we can limit our losses to around 10 percent, we can prepare ourselves psychologically—and mathematically. This way, we will not need to rely on disproportionate gains to make up for the loss; it's much easier to gain back 10 percent than 100 percent.

How can we limit our losses to 10 percent? We will look at that in later chapters, but for right now, understand that this is our goal.

One final point to remember about risk is that large losses or drawdowns will prevent us from achieving our goals. When we talked about time frames earlier, we talked about the importance of the timing of losses. Here, I've just extended the argument with the backing of math and psychology. This risk management tool is at the core of what I mean by putting seat belts on your portfolio.

HOW NOT TO FAIL

As Main Street investors, we want a simple portfolio that is inexpensive and minimizes drawdown risk, and we need to be able to manage it on the road in real life. Fortunately, we have the tools to do just that, and Wall Street has provided us with products that will allow us to meet our goals—products that are both inexpensive and good.

Asset classes and diversification

As you may have surmised by now, you will need two types of investments in your portfolio: stocks and bonds. Think of these as the two main wheels on your vehicle; much like a motorcycle, they should get you where you are headed.

Motorcycles are typically much faster than regular cars, but they also are more unsteady. A four-wheel car can handle conditions that a motorcycle can't, and it is steadier and more comfortable along the way. Fortunately, we can continue using the driving analogy, as we will be adding two more components to our portfolio: gold as an active holding and cash as a placeholder. These four wheels—stocks, bonds, gold, and cash—will drive our portfolio forward.

Let's take a more detailed look.

Stocks. We include stocks in our portfolios because we must; stocks are the only investment that can grow over time at a sustained rate higher than inflation.

That return comes as companies naturally grow with the economy. Over time, with economic growth and company growth, stocks have done better than any other asset class, and that is likely to continue.

The price we pay for this growth is volatility. Although returns have been strong over time, the stock market periodically pulls back, sometimes substantially, as we saw in 2000 and again in 2008. Most times, stocks will do very well; other times, they will get hit and get hit hard. Ideally, we want to own stocks when they're going up and not own them when they're going down. Unfortunately, it's not quite that simple. We must own stocks to meet our goals, but we also must figure out how to manage the risk of owning them—which is the subject of much of the rest of the book.

Bonds. Bonds are what companies and governments use to borrow money. When you buy a bond, you are making a loan. Like any loan, the borrower promises to make regular interest payments and then pay back the loan in full when it comes due. It is not quite as simple as this, but for our purposes, this definition covers the basics.

When we make a loan by purchasing a bond, we need to know two things:

1. What risks are we taking?
2. How much are we getting paid for those risks?

As always, let's start with risks. First is the risk that we will not get paid back, also known as *default risk*. Second is *interest rate risk*; if interest rates go up, the bonds you own will be worth less if you sell them. The flip side is also true: if interest rates go down, your bonds will be worth more. Interest rates have been declining for 30 years, and bonds have become very successful investments for this reason, but rates are about as low as they can go. What does that mean for us? We will come back to this.

The first reason you might use bonds in a portfolio is very simple: for income. With a solid borrower, you can be quite sure that you will get your interest payments on time and your money back at maturity. Higher-risk bonds, where you are less likely to get your interest and principal, pay more interest on your investment, as you might expect.

The problem with bonds is that the payment you get usually does not change over time, so it doesn't protect against inflation. Moreover, you are doubly exposed to inflation risk. If inflation rises, so will interest rates, which means the value of your bonds, if you must sell them, will go down. You end up with less purchasing power *and* less money. While the bond itself may be secure, your investment returns may not be.

Again, financial theory makes a good case for bonds. They have done very well for 30 years—while interest rates have been in decline. They have paid good income—but they pay much less now, due to lower interest rates. Bonds are, therefore, less relevant for income now than they have been historically.

The second reason for holding bonds in a portfolio—diversification—is a better one today and is the reason we will use. Bonds are perceived as lower-risk assets than stocks, so when stocks decline, investors often buy bonds, which drives prices up. This is exactly what we need to help manage our stock risk, so we will use bonds to help protect our portfolio. We will go into this in much more detail later. Overall, we should include bonds in our portfolio, but we will do so in a risk-managed way, and we won't use them primarily for income.

Gold. The third wheel on our car is gold. Gold has a bad reputation on Wall Street. What good does it do, goes the question? Can you eat it? Does it generate interest, earnings, or dividends? Where does your return come from?

These are good questions. Gold, in fact, gets its value solely from the fact that people want it. It doesn't generate a return; in fact, it costs money to hold. Gold has not been a mainstream holding for a long time, particularly in the U.S., due partially to the fact that private ownership of gold was illegal for much of the twentieth century.

I would also add that, at $1,000 per ounce or more, gold is not something the average investor can—or should—go out and buy. On the other hand, gold acts substantially differently from both stocks and bonds, so it can provide another layer of insurance for your portfolio. As we will see, owning gold at the right time can act as a very real seat belt in the event of a crash.

Stocks can get hit when the markets go south and people panic. Bonds tend to do well in similar circumstances, but when markets really panic, bonds can also get hit. Conversely, gold has often tended to go up in times of panic, and that is exactly when you need something that will zig when the rest of your portfolio zags. There are no guarantees, of course, but this is what has often happened in the past, such as during the crisis of 2008. Using a non-financial asset like gold can provide real protection when financial assets like stocks and bonds may not.

Buying and holding gold has problems of its own—transaction costs, storage costs, and security—for the average investor. Fortunately, Wall Street has come to the rescue, and you can now buy the equivalent of metallic gold in a form you can trade just like a stock. We will get into the details later, but for the moment, we want to include gold in our portfolio, and we can do so just like a stock.

Cash. The fourth wheel is cash. Cash is not a good place to be for long periods, but in the short term, cash can be wonderful. Being in cash buys you a couple of things:

1. Cash buys you protection from downturns. This allows you to sleep at night, to step aside if it looks like a problem is coming, and to wait for things to look better.
2. Cash buys what we call *optionality*. You can think of this as the right, but not the obligation, to take action later. If you go to cash, you can always buy back into stocks later with the same amount of cash you've had. You might lose some potential gains if the stock market goes up while you are in cash, but you won't really lose anything. You have an option to buy in, and you've taken an option to avoid losses.

We won't put money in cash very often. In fact, we don't want to be in cash at all, but we do want to have the option. Sometimes, we are more focused on not losing money rather than on how to make more. It is always possible to earn more returns in the future, but it's a lot harder to replace money lost. Remember that a 50-percent loss requires a 100-percent gain to break even. Sometimes, not losing money is the best way to make money—and cash lets us do that.

Market timing and seat belts

How do these pieces fit together? To put it simply, we are going to try to move out of the market when risk levels look high. To use our driving metaphor again, when ice starts building up, visibility is down, and driving becomes scarier, we are simply going to pull over and wait until conditions improve by selling out and sitting in cash.

This is, to put it mildly, not common practice in the investment world. Many would point out, correctly, that this would lower returns in bull markets. You can find statistics about how much lower your returns would have been had you missed the 10 best days in the market. The conventional argument is that it is simply not possible to predict crashes, and, therefore, it makes no sense to try to avoid them.

These arguments are sound—but they are beside the point. Let's take a step back and look at what we are trying to do here, which is lower risk, just as adding seat belts to a car does. No one today would argue against seat belts, but imagine what a car manufacturer in the 1950s, before seat belts were mandatory, might have said:

> "We can never predict when a car will be in a crash, and it is simply impossible to end all crashes; therefore, the idea of installing these new 'seat belts' is simply silly. Besides, if we add seat belts, the extra weight will slow down the car. Even then, in a severe enough accident, passengers would be injured regardless. No, driving is simply a risky business, and anyone in a car has to accept those risks."

The car manufacturer has some good points. We can't eliminate all auto accidents; this is true. It is also true that in some number of accidents, they will be bad enough that people will be injured or killed. It is even true that seat belts and other safety features add weight and cost to the car and do in fact slow it down a bit. Yet none of these facts takes into consideration that seat belts save thousands of lives every year. I would argue that investment portfolio safety precautions can have similar benefits.

Let's look at it from another perspective: it's impossible to predict the weather more than about a week ahead of time and nearly impossible to predict the path of, say, a hurricane even a couple of days ahead. Does that make weather predictions or hurricane warnings useless? Certainly not. When the potential damage is high enough, some kind of early warning and protective measures may well be worth it, even though there will be some cost involved. Overall, you may regret the times you put up hurricane shutters if the storm does not show, but when it does, your precautions will pay for all the times the storm passed you by.

We are not trying to increase our returns here—we probably will not—but to reduce our risk. Like a seat belt, these measures won't eliminate either the possibility of crashes or the risks we take, but they will substantially improve our odds of achieving our goals, which is all we are looking for.

The real risk: Not reaching your destination
We talked about risk. We talked about the different forms of return. Now we will talk about the real Main Street risk—that of not getting where we want to go. To do that, let's revisit our car trip analogy.

You are driving your son or daughter to college. You've planned the trip. You've packed the car. And now you set off.

School starts in three days, and you've carefully calculated the way to go, the amount of gas you will need, and where you are going to stay. One thing you neglected to consider, though, is that your car simply doesn't have the horsepower to pull the trailer up the hills on the way. You can't go fast enough to get where you're going when you want to get there.

This is a representation of return risk. If your portfolio doesn't have enough growth power to go up the hills you are going to face—in this case, inflation, which erodes purchasing power every year—it simply won't get there on time or perhaps at all. We must design our portfolios to have enough pulling power to get us to our goal.

What about drawdown risk? We can use the driving analogy here, too. Imagine the same trip, but now throw in a crash in the middle. If the car is damaged in a crash, good luck getting to college. If someone is hurt or killed, the problem is even worse. This is why we have well-designed cars, which can ride out a crash, and seat belts, to protect the occupants. Although a car crash, or a market crash, may be unavoidable, by both properly designing and adding seat belts, we maximize our chances of being able to complete our journey successfully.

The solution is the same for both cars and portfolios. You must design your portfolio, just like your car, to minimize the chances of catastrophic failure. (Remember the Ford Pinto? It was infamous for its poorly designed fuel tank, which led to fires and explosions in accidents.) Most cars are designed to work well in normal circumstances, on normal roads, in normal traffic. Likewise, diversification allows you to drive your portfolio through normal conditions.

This works most of the time, but the 2008 crisis put to rest the notion that diversification always works. The Main Street approach uses diversification, trusting the asset classes to do what they are supposed to in normal conditions. But it adds another layer of protection, incorporating a plan for when the whole system goes off track and adding some seat belts to protect us from the catastrophic crash.

Crash test your investments
We all remember the crash of 2008. It was not a one-time event. In fact, stock market crashes happen fairly regularly, so we need to plan for them like we would any other life event.

First, let's look at 1987. You may be old enough to remember it. It remains the largest single-day percentage crash in the U.S. markets. The Dow Jones Industrial Average dropped more than 25 percent. How could we defend against a downturn like this?

A conventional portfolio, say 60-percent stocks and 40-percent bonds, would have been exposed to a 15-percent drop in one day simply from its exposure to stocks. As you may remember from our earlier risk discussions, a 15-percent drop would require a larger recovery—in this case, 20 percent—to break even. More to the point, for individuals who retired in 1987, their entire retirement plan could have been crippled for decades by that one-time event. Just like the Ford Pinto car, a "Pinto" portfolio can experience catastrophic results in a crash.

In 2000, when the dot-com boom turned to bust, the Nasdaq technology stock index dropped by more than 60 percent and the S&P 500 by more than 40 percent. Many investors were exposed to tech stocks, so if they held 60 percent in the Nasdaq, for example—and many held more—they would have experienced a 36-percent drop in the portfolio as a whole. Note that it took 15 years for the Nasdaq to recover and pass its previous high. Even for a conservative investor in the S&P 500, the loss would have been almost 15 percent. Imagine if you were a college student preparing to start your freshman year or a new retiree in 2000.

In 2008, the S&P 500 dropped more than 50 percent. Again, for the conventional portfolio with a 60-percent weighting in stocks, that's a loss of more than 30 percent. As you can see, twice in the past 20 years—and three times in the past 30—the market has blown up in a way that could have destroyed the financial plans of many individuals, including retirees and college students.

These are scary numbers. They become even scarier when you consider that, in Wall Street terms, a 60/40 portfolio is moderately conservative. The target return on a portfolio like this is typically in the 8-percent range. Yet three times in the past 30 years, a moderately conservative portfolio has dropped between 15 percent and 30 percent.

This simply doesn't have to be the case, as we will see. What the average investor needs is a portfolio that has been crash tested—one that has seat belts to minimize our risk of blowing up. This is our goal, and this is what we will discuss in the coming chapters.

MAIN STREET INVESTING

We understand the risks, both from returns that are too low to meet our goals and from having a portfolio that can blow up and lose a disproportionate share of our hard-earned money. We understand how and why these risks work as they do. We understand that we must design a portfolio that is powerful enough to get us to our destination in a safe and timely fashion.

This is the easy part. What is much harder is to figure out how to do it. What I will do over the next several chapters is identify how you can avoid or contain the above risks; then, we'll construct a portfolio that will help you meet your goals.

Use the risk of failure as your guide

When we look at return risk, we know we need to find investments that will generate a return high enough to meet our goals. By and large, that means stocks. Despite the volatility, despite the risk, despite everything that comes with investing in the stock market, it's simply not optional. We will be in the stock market.

At the same time, we can't *only* be in the stock market. Stocks can underperform for a long period of time. There are times when you're better off being in the bond market, for example. But a one-asset portfolio is as stable as a unicycle, so we must look at other asset classes.

What we want from those other asset classes is protection from the downturn risk of stocks, as well as some supplemental return. As I discussed earlier, we will use bonds, gold, and cash as the moderating asset classes, as a four-wheeled car is inherently more stable than a unicycle, a motorcycle, or even a tricycle. Each of these asset classes provides unique characteristics that will make the portfolio as a whole work better than any of the individual investments.

By designing the portfolio specifically around the risks we face, we have taken the first steps in the Main Street investing approach.

Three core ideas

There are three core ideas behind implementing the Main Street approach:

1. **Make sure the costs you incur are both necessary and optimal.** No one goes to the lowest-priced doctor or lawyer. The lowest-cost products are not necessarily the best either, but you need to make sure you are getting value for your money. We will be choosing the investment tools that offer the biggest bang for the buck that we can find.

2. **It is possible to identify a potential train wreck before it happens and to step off the tracks.** Using a different analogy, suppose you live in Florida during hurricane season. When a storm warning comes in and a recommendation to evacuate is issued, you have a choice to make: Will you board up your house and leave, or will you stay put?

   Remember, weather forecasting—like market timing—is an uncertain art. You may evacuate only to see the storm turn away. Does that mean your effort was wasted? If the consequences are severe enough, you know it wasn't. Using a similar approach, we will look at how to get evacuation orders for your portfolio, so you can get out when the storm looks like it really will hit.

3. **Diversification works, but it is not the full story.** In normal times, we expect different types of investments to perform differently; by diversifying among them, we mitigate *unsystematic risk*. In 2008, however, we learned that when the system itself is at risk, many asset classes that are supposed to perform differently in theory may not do so in practice. So, we also need to add protection against *systematic risk* from problems with the system itself. These are the seat belts that can help protect you in the event of a crash.

Using these three ideas, we can build a portfolio that is much closer to a real Seat Belt Portfolio than anything now available. Let's get going.

HOW TO BUILD YOUR
INVESTMENT PORTFOLIO

Stocks and bonds

In the previous sections, we talked about why diversifying among asset classes makes sense. Here, we discuss how to do it, taking into account the three core ideas of Main Street investing—reasonable costs, the ability to step off the tracks, and real diversification.

The three ideas are somewhat at odds with one another. More diversification means more holdings, which means higher costs and more work when we step off—or back on—the tracks. What we need is a way to limit our holdings, diversify substantially, and do so at the lowest possible cost.

For stocks, you might argue that you want as many different ones as possible, including many smaller companies, which, in theory, should offer higher returns, since they tend to grow faster. That's one option, and it may be a good one. For our purposes, however, we are looking not only to participate in as much of the stock market gains as we can, but also to limit the potential risk of loss we face. Although they have the potential for higher returns, smaller-company stocks typically experience more volatility, which is to say they are riskier. They can and do go down much more than larger, more stable companies.

For this reason, we will use the S&P 500 as the basis of the Main Street investing approach to stocks. The S&P 500 represents the largest 500 publicly traded companies in the U.S. economy. These companies are financially solid; they pay dividends; and, by and large, they are stable. They also show a substantial record of growth over time. This group of stocks gives us the exposure and risk profile we want, fulfilling the diversification idea.

Just as the S&P 500 represents a broad cross-section of the U.S. economy and the U.S. business world, there's an equivalent index for bond investing called the Bloomberg Barclays U.S. Aggregate Bond Index. It includes a representative sample of fixed income investments, which is to say, bonds. The *Agg*, as it is known, is a benchmark against which many fixed income portfolios are judged.

When we invest in bonds, especially as Main Street investors, we face even bigger challenges than we do when we invest in stocks. First, bonds are different from stocks in that they trade in a very illiquid market, which means that prices for buyers and sellers can be substantially different. Unlike, say, IBM stock, where you can buy and sell in minutes at virtually the same price, IBM bonds may sell at prices substantially different from those at which you can buy. Second, while shares of stock in a company are generally the same, bonds can be very different. IBM may have one type of stock but almost 100 different types of bonds, each with different repayment terms and prices. The supply of each of those different types of bonds is also very limited.

It is, therefore, very hard to match the bond index by simply buying the right bonds. We also face the portfolio size problem. Because bonds typically trade at a minimum denomination of $1,000 or more, buying a diversified selection of bonds that matches the index can be difficult or impossible for the average investor. What we need is a way to get that diversified portfolio of bonds in a way that mirrors the index as closely as possible and enables us to do so in a cost-effective way. This would meet the diversification idea as well.

Note that for both stocks and bonds, our objectives are the same. We want a representative sample of each asset class, we want it to be broadly diversified, and we want it to be easily tradable. We also want it to be inexpensive.

For both of these asset classes, we have a solution—the *exchange-traded funds*, or *ETFs*, that track the respective indices. These products are exactly what they sound like—funds containing a specified group of assets, whether stocks or bonds or something else, that, unlike a mutual fund, can be bought and sold like a share of stock.

The ETF that represents the S&P 500, for example, allows you to buy a proportionate share of all 500 stocks in the index at the same time. You can do this as quickly, easily, and inexpensively as you can buy any share of stock. There are no limitations on tradability, there is full pricing transparency, and there typically are lower costs associated with the ETF.

Index mutual funds may also be an option. They offer similar investment strategies and may be cheaper to trade. The problem is that, historically, there have been restrictions on how frequently you can buy and sell without a penalty, and these restrictions can affect the Main Street strategy.

Because of this, I've chosen to use ETFs as the investing vehicle for Main Street investing. They best match Main Street investor needs, and they do it in the cheapest and easiest way available right now.

There are several products out there that will allow us to do exactly what we want. The most commonly traded ETF that replicates the S&P 500 is the **SPDR S&P 500 Trust ETF**, which trades under the symbol SPY. The most commonly traded bond ETF is the **iShares Core U.S. Aggregate Bond ETF**, and it trades under the symbol AGG. With just these two securities, we can build a portfolio that is more diversified than many portfolios out there.

Running the numbers

The question we must ask at this point is, does this approach work? It's a fair question. After all, as Yogi Berra said, "In theory there is no difference between theory and practice. In practice, there is."

One way to evaluate the Main Street investing approach is to look at a typical portfolio holding the two ETFs we chose, SPY and AGG, and match it against the performance of a similar mutual fund. If the ETF holdings are competitive, the performance should be similar. And that is just what we see in the following chart.

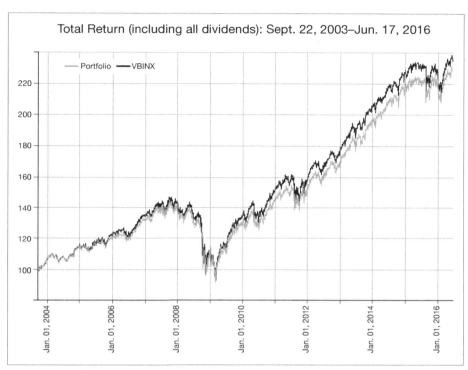

Total Return (including all dividends): Sept. 22, 2003–Jun. 17, 2016

Source: www.ETFreplay.com

Comparing a 60/40 portfolio of SPY and AGG with the Vanguard Balanced Index Fund (VBINX), which has a similar balanced allocation of stocks and bonds, we can see that the returns have been nearly identical over the past 10 years and more. Clearly, the theory behind Main Street investing works, in that a portfolio of ETFs can replicate the performance of a successful mutual fund.

If we are *only* looking to match the performance of the mutual fund over time, then it makes no sense to do the trading ourselves. We are better off just buying and holding the mutual fund. This is not a bad way to go, if we were to stop here.

It does not meet our objectives, however. Even with this portfolio, which is a good one, note that we had a drawdown of more than 30 percent in 2008. This kind of portfolio mix, although it may be cost effective and in other ways match the Main Street investing ideal, simply doesn't match the risk control goals we have set. Diversification between stocks and bonds alone is not going to get us where we need to go. So, what's the next step?

Gold

Sometimes, both the stock and bond markets go down together, so we need something that will do better when this happens.

Therefore, we need a different kind of asset. Stocks and bonds are both financial assets; they are priced via their value in currency, or, more precisely, their price is determined by the present value of the cash flows they will generate over time. When market conditions become uncertain, when a hurricane really starts to hit, investors lose faith in the future cash flows. They do not believe that companies will continue to generate the kinds of returns and profits they have been generating. They lose faith in companies' ability to pay off their bonds. They do not believe that the system is going to continue to grow. With that loss of faith, prices for both stocks and bonds decline together, just as we saw in 2008 and 2009. This is what we mean by systematic risk, the kind of risk that diversification does not protect against.

At times like these, what do investors believe? Or, to put it another way, what are investors looking for instead of financial assets? History shows us that at those times, investors are looking for something real, something that is immediately valuable, and something that will hold its value even more as things get worse. The classic example of this type of asset is gold.

What do we want from gold? We want an asset that will go up as other assets go down, especially in times of panic. We want an asset that is easily tradable. We want an asset that gives us both the benefit of a real asset and the tradability of a financial asset.

Gold, in and of itself, does not meet these requirements. If you have a safe deposit box full of gold coins, for example, they are risky: They can be lost or stolen, they are inconvenient to get to and expensive to sell or buy, and they are not easily integrated with the rest of your portfolio. Gold is also expensive and hard to acquire and store. What we need is something that acts like gold, is priced like gold, and works like gold but can be traded like a stock. In other words, just as with stocks and bonds, we need an ETF that holds gold. We will be using one of these ETFs, the **SPDR Gold Trust**, or GLD, in our portfolios.

We will be using it if, that is, it does what we want it to do when we crash test it. So, let's do that.

If you remember, our previous portfolio was 60-percent stocks and 40-percent bonds, which did well but had a 30-percent-plus drawdown in 2008. How can we put gold into the mix? We'll do the simplest thing possible and split the portfolio equally—one-third stocks, one-third bonds, and one-third gold. What happens then?

Let's look at real data. By the way, in both this chart and the one preceding, the time range encompasses the full range that the ETFs were available to be traded. The reason the time period in the chart below is slightly shorter than in the previous chart is because GLD was created later than SPY and AGG. ETFs are a relatively recent creation and, therefore, can be tested back only to the date they were first launched.

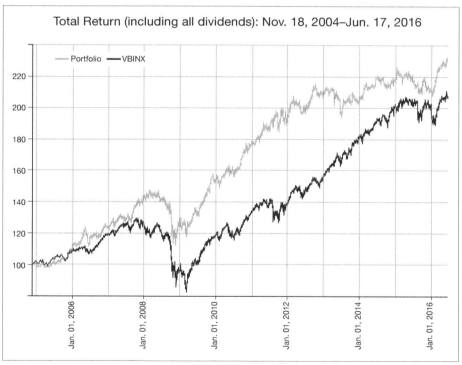

Source: www.ETFreplay.com

As you can see, putting gold, in the form of the gold ETF, GLD, into the portfolio during this time made a substantial difference in performance. As we did in the previous section, we are comparing our portfolio with a low-cost mutual fund, VBINX, which has 60-percent stocks and 40-percent bonds.

Let's think about what happened here. We have fewer stocks—just 33 percent instead of 60 percent. We have fewer bonds—33 percent instead of 40 percent. And we have gold—an asset that is often not included in many portfolios. And yet, we have substantially improved not only our absolute returns, but also our drawdown during the financial crisis. We have limited our worst losses to 25 percent, down from 30 percent. We made more money and took less risk. Clearly, including gold in a portfolio meets the Main Street objectives.

Cash

Are we done yet? Perhaps not. What would happen if we included cash or, in this case, very short-term government bonds, which are substantially equivalent to cash? Would that help? Well, let's look at the chart on the next page, where we consider a portfolio that is equally divided among stocks, bonds, gold, and cash.

Adding cash as an asset class brought mixed results. Returns went down, but so did risk. The maximum drawdown went from about 25 percent to about 17 percent. Cash obviously has value as a risk reducer, but is it worth giving up returns to reduce the risk? We will talk about this more in the next section.

Where are we now?

Let's summarize where we are now. We looked at four asset classes: stocks, bonds, gold, and cash. We reviewed why they should be part of the portfolio. And we built some portfolios to test our assumptions and see what effect each of the different asset classes had on performance.

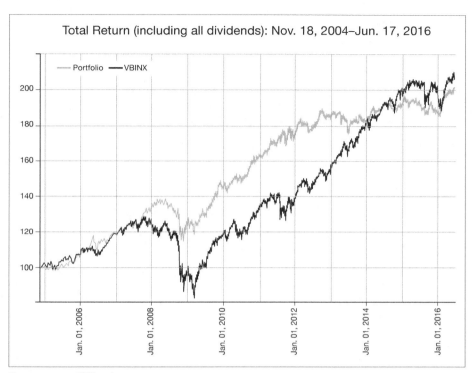

Total Return (including all dividends): Nov. 18, 2004–Jun. 17, 2016

Source: www.ETFreplay.com

From a Main Street perspective, I would argue that we are getting there. Here's a recap of our objectives:

1. **Slow failure or return risk:** If you look at the charts, the returns of many of our models have matched or exceeded those of the 60-percent stocks/40-percent bonds portfolio, VBINX, which represents what is usually considered a portfolio suitable for a broad range of people. If we can match that portfolio, we are matching the typical expectations for the average person. In fact, as noted, we are beating them.

2. **Fast failure or drawdown risk:** We have managed to significantly reduce the drawdown risk of the portfolio compared with the 60/40 version while matching or exceeding the returns. If we can match the returns with reduced risk, we are beating Wall Street expectations.

3. **The sleep-at-night factor:** To get a good grip on this factor, let's think about the period over which we ran these analyses. The time period covers the great financial crisis, the worst economic and financial earthquake in the world since 1929. Knowing your model performed well, and limited risk, during the most difficult market period in the past 80 years has to help with this one.

4. **The lifestyle goal:** Main Street investors have lives; they do not want and shouldn't have to spend all their time managing their investments. What we did here was simply rebalance the portfolios monthly—12 times a year—and we still managed to meet and beat the standard example. As Main Street investors, we looked at the 60/40 mutual fund in the examples above and said we must do substantially better in order to justify taking a different approach. I would argue that, even at this stage, we have done just that and that the cost of perhaps one hour per month is justified by the reduced risk and potentially enhanced returns we have seen.

This analysis is not finished, though. We have a lot more work to do. First—and this is important—we need to see if there's any real-world verification of our ideas. We will do that next.

Second, even if the ideas are supported in the real world, we need to ask ourselves how these ideas can fail. How does this approach blow up? If you do not understand how and why something can fail, you do not fully understand the risks. As Main Street investors, we need to subject our ideas to a very clear analysis of where the risks are. We will do that by crash testing our portfolio.

IF YOU'RE SO SMART . . .

What we have done so far is experiment with different asset classes in different mixes to see if we could develop a portfolio that met our Main Street investing objectives. Of course, this begs the question: if this approach works, why aren't more people doing it?

The Permanent Portfolio

It's a fair question. In fact, people are doing similar things and have been for some time. In September 1999, a man named Harry Browne published a book called *Fail-Safe Investing*, in which he outlined what he called the Permanent Portfolio idea. It was simple; it consisted of 25-percent stocks, 25-percent bonds, 25-percent gold, and 25-percent cash. At the time, it was revolutionary—professional financial people ridiculed it—but when you look at how it would have performed over time, it did incredibly well.

Browne looked at the performance of his ideas across U.S. history, and he and other authors also analyzed the ideas in other countries and times. Across the board, the portfolio resulted in smoother, less volatile, and higher returns than many conventional portfolios. What made the portfolio work was the universality of the underlying ideas—that stocks are high return but risky, that bonds are medium return and less risky, that gold has universal appeal in times of trouble, and that cash not only smooths out returns, but also lets you buy in when values decline. Even though it contradicted both financial theory and Wall Street wisdom, the idea worked well for the average investor across multiple decades and markets.

The Permanent Portfolio is very similar to the final portfolio we designed above. That's no accident; I read *Fail-Safe Investing* several years ago, and it started me on a course of research that has resulted in the book you hold your hands.

What makes Browne's work relevant to our discussion right now, when we are talking about whether the Main Street investing approach works in real life, is that Browne was a founder of a mutual fund based on this idea, launched in 1982, well before he published his book. The fund was called, appropriately enough, the Permanent Portfolio Fund, and it trades under the symbol PRPFX. It's a great example of how a Main Street idea was turned into a real investment product, one that continues to do well to this day.

The idea and the mutual fund

The Permanent Portfolio Fund is interesting for a couple of reasons. It didn't exactly implement Harry Browne's idea, but it was close—close enough that it was a fair test of whether an idea like his, using real diversification, could yield real, stable returns over time and whether theoretical, tested results could continue in the real world.

The differences between the fund and Browne's ideas also speak to the differences between theory and practice. Unlike Browne, for example, the fund didn't try to get the whole stock market, just a subset of it. Also unlike Browne, it didn't hold just gold but a mix of gold, silver, and stable currencies. The differences are consistent with Browne's basic ideas, but they are different. Nonetheless, the fact that the fund was based on an attempt at real diversification among these categories provides a test of whether this kind of approach can work in the real world over time.

The Permanent Portfolio Fund had a slow start. It was doing something—much like we are in this book—that Wall Street was not used to and did not particularly like. In fact, it went against much of the prevailing financial orthodoxy of the time. Investors and the general public were, unsurprisingly, slow to take it up. Financial investors and Wall Street were even slower to take it up. Inflows—that is, the amount that investors put into the fund—grew very slowly over time.

That all changed with the financial crisis. The Permanent Portfolio Fund performed as advertised, as you can see from the following chart. It did much better during and after the crisis than many balanced funds. The reason for this was the inclusion of gold. In fact, after the crisis, the Permanent Portfolio Fund attracted billions of dollars in inflows and was named a top-performing fund by mutual fund research company Morningstar. The ideas, radical at the time, were validated not only by performance but also by investor dollars and recognition by one of the major fund-rating companies.

Given the differences between the idea and the fund as implemented, however, is the fund a good expression of the underlying theories?

Let's test that. The easiest way is to compare the performance of PRPFX with the final model we created in the previous chapter.

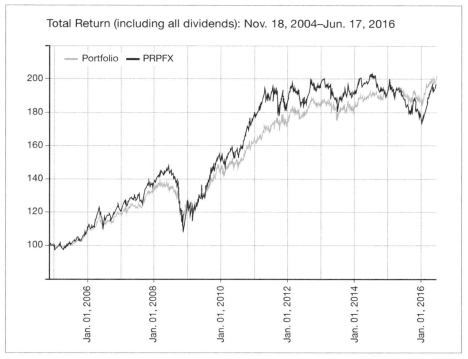

Source: www.ETFreplay.com

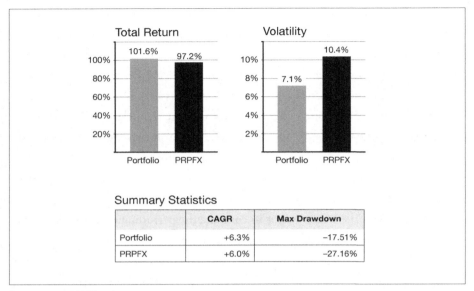

Summary Statistics

	CAGR	Max Drawdown
Portfolio	+6.3%	−17.51%
PRPFX	+6.0%	−27.16%

Source: www.ETFreplay.com

CAGR is the compounded annual growth rate (i.e., the annual return). The max drawdown is from maximum levels before the drawdown.

We can see a couple of things from this chart. First, our portfolio has indeed performed similarly to the Permanent Portfolio Fund, lending important real-world verification. Second, for the work we have done, the extra return is not that great, so it feels like wasted effort. What does justify using our approach, however, is that our portfolio lost a maximum of about 18 percent at any given time while the Permanent Portfolio Fund lost more than 27 percent at its worst. This is a big difference, and it's large enough to help prevent fast failure in our portfolios, which is the goal.

So, we can conclude that the underlying ideas have worked, both in theory and in practice, which gives me confidence in our approach. As to whether the results are good enough to meet our Main Street goals, you can draw your own conclusion. Personally, I think we can do better. Returns over this period almost match our requirements, so we are getting there, but the maximum drawdown, at almost 18 percent, is still much greater than our goal of 10 percent. I not only think we can do better, I think we *must*. There's no denying, though, that the

Permanent Portfolio Fund is a very good potential option for the buy-and-hold Main Street investor. You can do better doing it yourself, but this may be a good option if you don't want to.

Adding seat belts: Using moving averages to reduce risk

Let's look at specifics here. We know that real diversification can work, but it may not protect you in a really big crash. We saw that in 2008. Ideally, what we need is a way to identify when the market is at risk, so we can use that knowledge to implement the third Main Street idea—being able to step aside. In other words, we want to use our seat belts when a crash looks likely.

Fortunately, there is a simple idea that can help us do this: the moving average.

What is a *moving average*? A moving average is the average price of a security over a certain period. If I talk about a 50-day moving average for the S&P 500, for example, I am referring to the average closing price of the index over the most recent 50-day period.

This is useful because it provides a basis to compare what's happening now with what happened in the recent past. The theory is that if prices are higher than they have been in the recent past, then the market is going up, and vice versa. If the market looks like it will continue to go up, you probably want to buy; if the market is going down, you probably want to sell.

Of course, it's not quite that simple. If it were, we could all be billionaires simply by looking at stock prices on the Internet and buying and selling when the moving averages trend.

In fact, many signals are false alarms. So, any attempt to use moving averages has to separate the real signals from the false ones. How can we do that?

One way is to check the averages using different time frames: daily, weekly, or monthly, for example. Another is to vary the length of the trend you are looking at: 50, 100, and 200 days are typical trend lengths.

My own work has shown that using a longer moving average period, and evaluating it once a month, is the best match between real signals and false alarms. It is not perfect, but it has been remarkably successful over time. The following charts, and the rest of the analysis, will be based on monthly figures and updates, as this time frame provides the best results overall.

To see what I mean, let's look at the data. This chart takes us back 20 years. During that time, we have had two significant downturns—in 2000 and 2008—and any signal should have caught both fairly near the top. The dark line in this chart is a 10-month, or 200-day, moving average, and the light line is the S&P 500 stock index. The data is evaluated once a month; at that point, an investor would be invested if the index is above the average or in cash if it is below.

You can see that the 10-month moving average signaled to get out of the market just after the peak in both 2000 and 2007, as marked by the top arrows. These are the points where the S&P 500 dropped below its 200-day moving average. Had you listened to this indicator, you would have saved yourself a lot of money. You would have missed the big declines, which is consistent with our goal of containing losses.

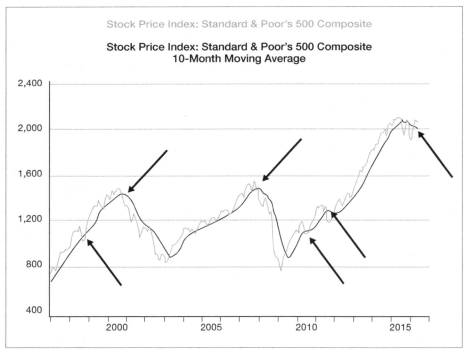

Source: Standard & Poor's, Haver Analytics

Unfortunately, however, you would also have gotten false signals. In 1998, several times in the mid-2000s, and in 2010, 2011, and 2015, you would have seen the index, the light line, drop below the moving average and then bounce back above it, without a serious decline. With these false signals, shown by the bottom arrows, you would have had to sell out and then buy back in at a potentially higher price.

> **A Note About Moving Averages**
> The **10-month** and **200-day** moving averages are essentially the same thing; they differ primarily in how they can be applied. The 200-day figure allows you to make changes daily, whereas the 10-month figure is designed for monthly updates.

Clearly, the 10-month, or 200-day, moving average is not a perfect signal, but it did work for the two big events over this 20-year period. And even given the false alarms, if you had listened to those two genuine signals, in 2000 and 2008, you would have been significantly ahead overall.

For fewer false signals, we can look at a longer-term moving average. Let's see what a 20-month, or 400-day, moving average looks like.

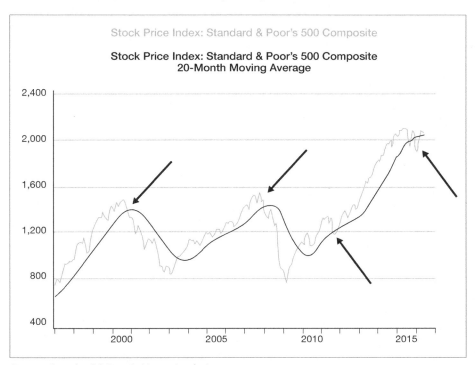

Source: Standard & Poor's, Haver Analytics

As with the 10-month moving average, we can see that we did indeed catch the two big events, although we would have lost more off the top—see the larger gap between the peak of the index and where it crosses the dark line—than we did with the 10-month moving average. This is the trade-off—a slower reaction but fewer false alarms. In fact, with the 20-month moving average, we have only three false alarms—one in 2011 and two in 2015—rather than the multiple false alarms we had with the 10-month moving average.

When we consider the choice of more false alarms versus a greater potential drop, I find the prospect of a greater drawdown to be more worrisome, given our Main Street investor objectives, than the increased trading activity created by false alarms. We will, therefore, be using the 10-month, or 200-day, moving average for the rest of this book, accepting the risk of more false alarms in exchange for potentially smaller losses off the top.

ADDING SEAT BELTS
TO YOUR PORTFOLIO

The obvious next step is to combine the real diversification portfolio with the seat belt effect of the moving average analysis. Before we do that, though, we need to consider the impact of moving average analysis on the individual asset classes.

Stocks and moving averages

This will be a short section that essentially recaps what we talked about earlier. Let's repeat the charts and take a closer look.

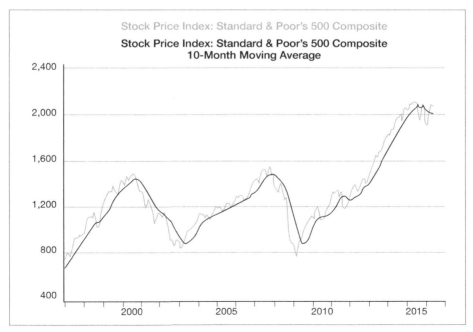

Source: Standard & Poor's, Haver Analytics

In theory, over the past 20 years, using the 10-month moving average as a signal to get out of the market has achieved our objective of limiting losses when the market turns down. As we discussed before, it caught the two major turning points, though it came at the cost of several false alarms.

Worth noting is something that is not included in the chart. In 1987, with a crash in October, the 10-month moving average would have completely missed it. We will talk about that when we get to the crash test analysis, but just remember that the moving average is by no means a failsafe indicator.

Since we are going to be using ETFs, let's test the moving average analysis approach using real ETF results.

Let's talk about the chart on the next page for a minute, as it shows all of the factors we have discussed so far. The top chart shows the SPY ETF versus its 10-month moving average. Below that, the equity curve shows how much money an investor would have had, starting with $100, if he or she had followed this strategy. Next are six windows that show, respectively:

- The proportion of times the strategy was right (winning) versus wrong (losing)
- The size of the gain on the median right decision versus wrong decision
- The total return of the strategy versus the index
- The average amount of time a right decision was held versus a wrong decision
- The longest sequence of right and wrong decisions
- The largest drawdown from a prior peak

This last item is the one we are focusing on most.

You can see here that applying a 10-month moving average strategy (i.e., the backtest information on the charts) to the SPY ETF (which, remember, holds the stocks in the S&P 500 Index) over this period resulted in much higher returns (204 percent vs. 101 percent) and much lower drawdown risk (16.6 percent versus 50.8 percent) than just buying and holding. Returns were more than double over this period, whereas the worst drawdown was only one-third that of the buy-and-hold approach. Clearly, applying the moving average strategy to real data has produced favorable results.

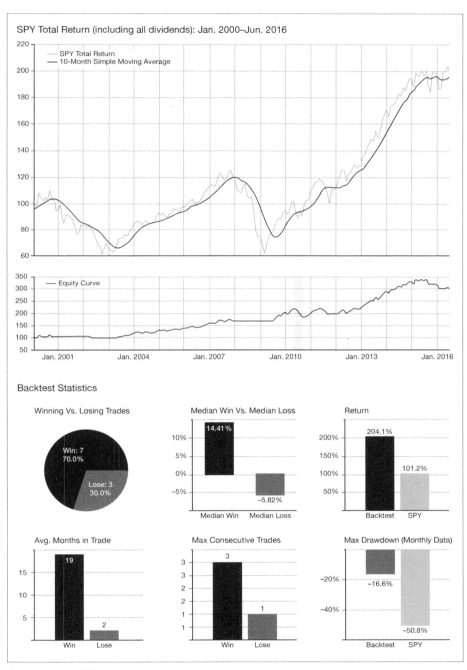

SPY Total Return (including all dividends): Jan. 2000–Jun. 2016

Backtest Statistics

Note also that this test covers the two major crashes over the past 20 years, in 2000 and 2008. Right now, with stock market valuations high again, this suggests the moving average method might well be as timely now as it was then.

Let's look at bonds now.

Bonds and moving averages

Unlike stocks, which have moved up and down in big swings over the past 20 years, bonds have been in an almost uninterrupted bull market. That is to say, bond prices have increased as interest rates have dropped. It will, therefore, be interesting to see what a moving average analysis applied to bonds shows us. Let's go to the long-term history chart first, where you can see how small the bond drawdowns have been compared with those of stocks.

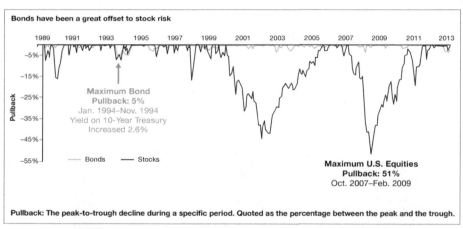

Source: http://blog.helpingadvisors.com/2013/11/07/bond-bashing-like-its-1999/

Morningstar monthly maximum drawdown percentage for the Bloomberg Barclays U.S. Aggregate Bond Index (Bonds) and the Russell 3000® Index (Stocks) from December 31, 1989, to September 30, 2013. Indices are unmanaged, and investors cannot invest directly in an index. Index returns represent past performance, are not a guarantee of future performance, and are not indicative of any specific investment.

Now let's look at the more recent data and track how our chosen bond product, the AGG ETF, performed.

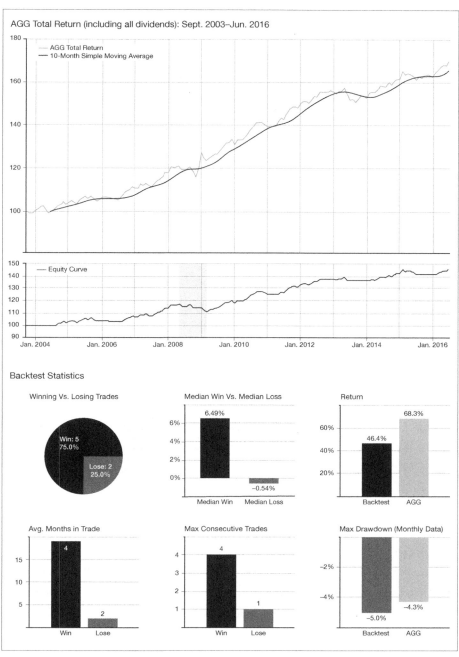

AGG Total Return (including all dividends): Sept. 2003–Jun. 2016

Backtest Statistics

Source: www.ETFreplay.com

Unlike with stocks, you can see that using a moving average analysis has not worked with bonds over the past decade or so. Total returns were lower, at 46 percent versus 68 percent, and the maximum drawdown was actually higher, at 5 percent versus 4.3 percent. Why? There simply have not been any major drawdowns where a moving average strategy would have protected against a large loss. Compared with the buy-and-hold approach, the moving average analysis resulted in lower overall returns, and the drawdown was worse. Should we use a moving average approach for bonds?

Not if you look at the historical data. Before we decide not to, though, let's look at the bigger picture. The past 30 years have seen a sustained bull market for bonds. Unlike stocks, there have been no significant drawdowns. In that kind of market, as financial theory suggests and as my tests show to be true, buy-and-hold is the way to go.

Further backing up this argument, because bonds pay cash flows in the form of interest payments over time, you would sacrifice those interest payments by being out of the market. In addition, bonds have tended to be much less volatile over time than stocks, suggesting that the costs of trading the bonds will not be offset by any greater returns going forward.

These are good arguments, and they may end up being correct. The problem is that the 30-year bull market in bonds, driven by the decline in interest rates that has generated those consistently positive returns, may not continue much longer. Interest rates have been declining for the past three decades, but at the end of 2015, the Federal Reserve raised rates for the first time in many years and has continued to make additional small increases since then. It remains to be seen how much more rates will increase—or when—but the prospect of higher interest rates is very real.

More to the point, we as Main Street investors are not just looking at the next year but at the next decade and even beyond. Over that time frame, interest rate increases are almost certain, which will probably end the bull market in bonds, possibly in a sudden and damaging way.

The other factor suggesting that being able to move out of the bond market is not such a bad idea is the very low level of current interest rates. The amount of interest bonds pay is based on interest rates, and with rates as low as they are, those payments are also low. You, therefore, give up much less in the way of return by moving out of the market than you would have historically.

There are good arguments both ways, with no clear answer in sight. In the best Main Street fashion, we must, therefore, look at both buy-and-hold and tactical methods when we construct a portfolio and see what conclusions we can draw. At the end of the day, having looked at both options, we must decide whether we prefer higher returns with more potential drawdown risk or lower potential returns along with lower potential for a drawdown.

Now let's look at gold.

Gold and moving averages

We look at the performance of gold by itself, as shown by the GLD ETF, in the chart on the following page. Here, we can clearly see that from 2005 to 2012 (i.e., before and after the 2008 financial crisis), gold benefited any portfolio. In early 2012, however, gold started to decline, and from then until recently, gold has subtracted from overall returns, with the worst damage occurring in 2014.

Using moving averages didn't help during this period either. Total returns are worse using moving averages, and while the drawdown is better, it is still unacceptable. Given that and the extended drawdown from 2012 through 2015, if we look at gold on an asset class basis alone, it's fair to conclude that investing in gold doesn't make a lot of sense.

There are two interesting things about this analysis, though. First, gold did very well during the crisis period, even as financial assets like stocks and bonds took a hit. This suggests that gold acted exactly as we hoped it would, when we needed it to—as insurance. Therefore, gold does have a place in our portfolio. We don't expect to make money on insurance, after all, but we need it as a cushion in difficult times. Second, and equally as important, is how the moving average approach failed in the short term (i.e., in 2014 and 2015). Remember, part of the Main Street investing approach is to understand when something doesn't work and why.

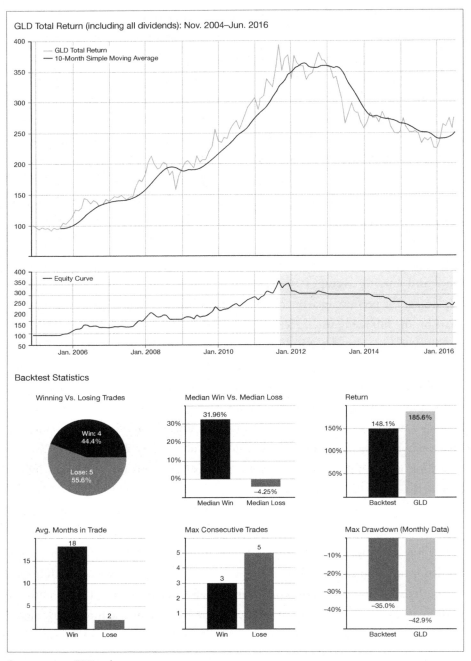

GLD Total Return (including all dividends): Nov. 2004–Jun. 2016

Backtest Statistics

Winning Vs. Losing Trades

Median Win Vs. Median Loss

Return

Avg. Months in Trade

Max Consecutive Trades

Max Drawdown (Monthly Data)

Source: www.ETFreplay.com

If you look at 2014 and 2015, you see that gold was bouncing around, moving up and down seemingly at random. There was no trend, and that is exactly when moving average analysis fails. If you look at the return from 2006 through 2012, where there was a strong trend, you see that the moving average approach worked quite well.

Overall, the short-term data raises a question as to whether gold should be included in our portfolio. Over the longer term, particularly around the financial crisis, the performance of gold strongly supports its inclusion, a point we will come back to when we develop the actual portfolios. When we consider gold on its own, the conclusion is not as clear; when we consider it as part of a portfolio, the result speaks for itself.

How does this fit with our Main Street objectives?

We are now at the point where we have laid out the foundation for the rest of our approach. We have defined the objectives. We have gone through the major ideas we are going to use—the asset classes: stocks, bonds, gold, and cash—and the two strategies we are going to employ when using those asset classes—real diversification and adding seat belts. What remains is to think about how this fits into our goals. The better we understand why our tools fit our need for risk management, the better able we will be to move through the rest of the discussion.

The final thing to review here is the core objective of Main Street investing: to get acceptable returns, and avoid slow failure risk, without the most damaging form of fast failure risk—drawdowns. Everything we do here is designed to make enough money to achieve our goals, while minimizing the chance of losing a lot of money at any point in the process. Gold is in the portfolio because it can help us avoid losing money when everything else is going down. Stocks are in the portfolio to make money over time, but we also use moving averages to avoid as much downside as we can. Bonds are in the portfolio because, over time, they've been a good investment, so they can make us money, but they will also help offset the losses from stocks. Cash is in there to preserve our purchasing power, as well as to provide buying power when markets go down.

THE SEAT BELT
PORTFOLIO IN PRACTICE

Now let's put all the pieces together. We talked about our objectives. We talked about our assets. We talked about the tools we are going to use. Now it's time to put them all together and see what happens.

We will do this step by step. We will present each piece as we go and see how it affects returns. In many ways, this is going to mirror what we did earlier, but this time, by adding the seat belt layer, we should be able to see exactly what benefit it provides.

We are going to start by looking at the past 11-plus years, starting in 2005 (the year all our ETFs became available) and ending in mid-2016, as I was first writing this book. This is a meaningful timespan for our test, as it had both booms and busts, from the good times of the mid-2000s, to the financial crisis in 2008–2009, and then to the ongoing recovery.

If you remember, though, we talked about how ideas have to be tested over multiple periods. Strategies that work in one era may not work in another. So, after testing the strategy using data from the past 11 years, we will go back and look at how our Seat Belt Portfolio performed over the 30 years from 1983 to 2013. The time frame here comes from when I originally developed this idea, conducting a 30-year analysis based on the data that was available.

This 30-year period really is a useful time frame over which to evaluate a strategy. Thirty years certainly covers any college savings period, as well as most people's retirement. Not only that, it also covers multiple economic and market cycles. If the strategy worked over the past 10 years, and over the 20 years before that, we can have more confidence in the results over the next 20 or 30 years as well.

After doing the 30-year review, we will go through the results in detail. As promised, we will look at troubled times—1987, 2000, and 2008—to see exactly how the portfolio performed. Crash testing a portfolio can provide invaluable insight. In our case, if we can understand how and why the portfolio performed the way it did in those years, it will give us more confidence in its performance going forward.

Putting the pieces together
First, some housekeeping. All the following charts will look at the performance of various ETFs or funds.

- For **stocks**, we will be using SPY, which replicates the S&P 500 in an ETF form.
- For **bonds**, we will be using AGG, which replicates the Bloomberg Barclays U.S. Aggregate Bond Index, again in ETF form.
- For **gold**, we'll use GLD, which is an ETF that holds gold.
- For **cash**, we'll use SHY, an ETF that holds very short-term government securities and is as close to risk free as you can get in a financial asset—much like cash.

Note that other ETFs and mutual funds may do the same thing as those I am using here. The ones I have selected are good tools, which is why I am using them, but you do have other options.

Having selected these tools, we will then take our portfolio in steps, adding one asset at a time and charting the results. Each chart will compare the performance of the portfolio using the moving average signals against the performance of a benchmark asset, which will be explained in the appropriate section.

Let's start out with stocks. Because we are using the S&P 500 as our stock holding, represented by the SPY ETF, the graph on page 60 shows how the moving average approach to that ETF does compared with buying and holding the ETF.

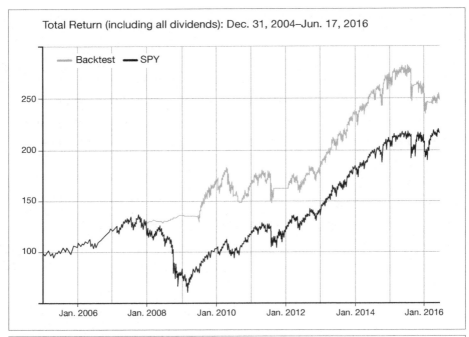

Total Return (including all dividends): Dec. 31, 2004–Jun. 17, 2016

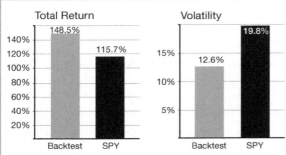

Summary Statistics

	CAGR	Max Drawdown
Backtest	+8.3%	−18.7%
SPY	+6.9%	−55.2%

Trades	25
Total Periods	138
Total Days	2,885

Winning periods	93	(67.4%)	Losing periods	45	(32.6%)
Periods outperformed benchmark	14	(10.1%)	Periods underperformed benchmark	15	(10.9%)
Best period		+7.46%	Worst period		−7.95%
Median winning period		+1.70%	Median losing period		−1.82%

Source: www.ETFreplay.com

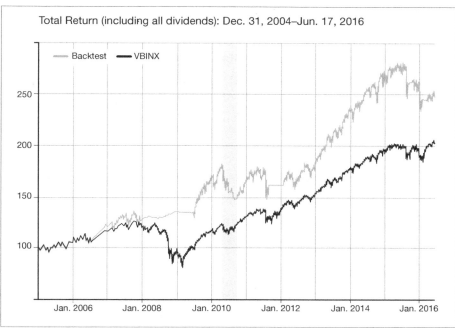

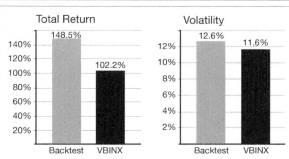

Summary Statistics

	CAGR	Max Drawdown
Backtest	+8.3%	−18.7%
VBINX	+6.3%	−36.0%

Trades	25
Total Periods	138
Total Days	2,885

Winning periods	93	(67.4%)	Losing periods	45	(32.6%)
Periods outperformed benchmark	79	(57.2%)	Periods underperformed benchmark	59	(42.8%)
Best period		+7.46%	Worst period		−7.95%
Median winning period		+1.70%	Median losing period		−1.82%

Source: www.ETFreplay.com

Note that until January 2008, the two lines overlap. There were no drops below the moving average, so the two approaches were identical. In 2008, of course, the market dropped, and there the two approaches diverge.

From 2005 through mid-2016, buying and holding the SPY ETF (the dark line), which tracks the S&P 500, offered a return of just under 7 percent per year. The maximum drawdown was more than 55 percent during the great financial crisis.

Now let's turn to the moving average approach (the light line). Using a 10-month moving average to move in and out of the market, evaluated monthly, we got an annual return of more than 8 percent (better than the buy-and-hold approach) and did so with a maximum drawdown risk of 18.7 percent, about one-third that of the buy-and-hold approach.

Using our moving average strategy (i.e., seat belts) did more than improve performance against the buy-and-hold approach. It also resulted in superior performance when compared with buying and holding a standard balanced portfolio.

In the chart on page 61, the dark line represents a buy-and-hold strategy for the mutual fund VBINX, which holds a mix of 60-percent stocks and 40-percent bonds. Here, we can see that our Seat Belt Portfolio (the light line) had higher returns and lower risk than the diversified Wall Street 60/40 portfolio over the same period.

I point this out to demonstrate the value, even at a simple level, of including seat belts in a portfolio. Not only does it not hurt performance, it improves it. If you think about it, what this chart shows is that using a simple moving average approach as a seat belt provided more risk reduction, over the past 10 years, than the conventional diversification approach. It also generated higher returns.

This isn't to say that diversification does not add value; it does, and we will use it, but it is incomplete by itself. In fact, we get better results by using both diversification and seat belts, and the results get even better as we diversify further. Let's look at what happened when we added bonds as 40 percent of the portfolio. In the chart on the following page, the light line is 60-percent stocks (SPY) and 40-percent bonds (AGG).

Total Return (including all dividends): Dec. 31, 2004–Jun. 17, 2016

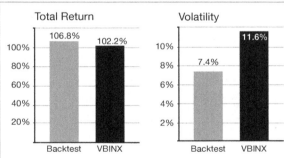

Summary Statistics

	CAGR	Max Drawdown		Trades	25
Backtest	+6.6%	–10.2%		Total Periods	138
VBINX	+6.3%	–36.0%		Total Days	2,885

Winning periods	93	(67.4%)	Losing periods	45	(32.6%)
Periods outperformed benchmark	66	(47.8%)	Periods underperformed benchmark	72	(52.2%)
Best period		+4.98%	Worst period		–4.36%
Median winning period		+1.22%	Median losing period		–1.06%

Source: www.ETFreplay.com

Total Return (including all dividends): Dec. 31, 2004–Jun. 17, 2016

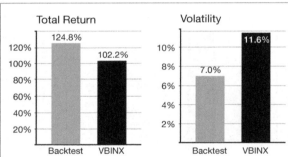

Total Return

Volatility

Summary Statistics

	CAGR	Max Drawdown
Backtest	+7.3%	–9.5%
VBINX	+6.3%	–36.0%

Trades	85
Total Periods	138
Total Days	2,885

Winning periods	88	(63.8%)	Losing periods	50	(36.2%)
Periods outperformed benchmark	66	(47.8%)	Periods underperformed benchmark	72	(52.2%)
Best period		+6.74%	Worst period		–3.46%
Median winning period		+1.23%	Median losing period		–1.05%

Source: www.ETFreplay.com

As expected, adding bonds dropped our return—from 8.3 percent to 6.6 percent—but our drawdown risk dropped by almost half—from 18.7 percent to only 10.2 percent. Think about that; over the past 10 years, we would have lost, at most, about 10 percent, top to bottom, at any given time. That is consistent with our target maximum loss of 10 percent, which suggests that this portfolio meets our goals. We are done!

Well, not really, but we're getting close. Let's look at what happens if we add gold to the mix. This next portfolio on page 64 (again represented by the light line) has 34-percent SPY, 33-percent AGG, and 33-percent GLD.

Adding gold to the portfolio increased returns—from 6.6 percent to 7.3 percent and decreased drawdown risk—from 10.2 percent to 9.5 percent. The risk-adjusted performance was once again better than the 60/40 portfolio. Diversification continues to add value, but the combination of seat belts and diversification continues to do best of all.

10 years of data is good; 30 years is better

Now that we have analyzed the results of the past 10 years and validated our model, can we be assured that this process works? The short answer is no. You could argue that the past 10 years have in fact been exceptional and not representative of the long term, and you would have a good case. The great financial crisis was one of the worst crashes in history. Arguably, to take any period that includes the worst crash in history is to say it is not representative.

Although I won't replicate all the previous charts, we need to determine whether the results from the previous 10-year period are comparable with those from the past 30 years. To do that, we will look at returns, drawdowns, and some other risk metrics.

The real benefit here is that we will also have enough data to draw some meaningful conclusions about the average returns we can expect over longer periods. As savers and investors, we are not that interested in the results of any one year, as long as it's not too bad. What we *are* interested in is the average return, as well as the minimum return, we can expect over our time horizon. Those are the numbers that determine whether we reach our goal.

For college savers, the appropriate time horizon is probably around 10 years or so. For most parents, 10 years approximates the savings period for a child between 5 and 10 years of age, although for a newborn, a 20-year horizon is appropriate. For retirement savers, your immediate horizon is also probably between 10 and 20 years, although it often extends beyond that. In both cases, if we have enough data to meaningfully consider what our 10- to 20-year returns are likely to be, that helps our planning significantly.

The models in our 30-year analysis are somewhat different from the models we have looked at so far. We have been able to use ETFs to generate the 10-year results, but many of them did not exist before about 2005, so we'll be using index numbers in this next analysis.

The 30-year analysis also uses slightly different assumptions about allocations between asset classes. This is deliberate, in that it allows us to test whether the model is vulnerable to small changes in the assumptions. One characteristic of weak models is that the results change even with a small alteration in the starting conditions. As it turns out—again, fortunately—the Main Street model generated substantially similar results under varying initial conditions, showing it is robust. So, these models serve as a check on each other in multiple ways.

The Seat Belt model results can be summarized as follows:

Time Period	Average Return	Max Drawdown
30 years	9.46%	−11.43%
20 years	9.88%	−8.32%
10 years	9.93%	−8.32%
5 years	10.60%	−7.45%

If you compare these numbers with those of the final Seat Belt Portfolio we ended up with on page 64, they are quite consistent, lending credibility to both analyses. Even the differences support the models. We see slightly higher returns in the 30-year models, compared with the previous one, because the 10-year model uses ETF returns, which include low but real costs, while the 30-year data is based on index returns, which do not include these costs. Over time, such as during the past five years when stocks have done well, this is exactly what you should expect to see.

Just as the two models support and reinforce each other, the fact that the observed results are extremely similar suggests that the model works the same way over different periods, which is one of the crucial tests. The average return has stayed between 9 percent and 10 percent for the past 30 years. The maximum drawdown has also been incredibly consistent. Clearly, this method has the same applicability over the past 10 years as it has over the past 30.

Think about this for a second. We developed a model using proven techniques and applied it to the past 10 years of real-world data, where it worked. Arguably, the past 10 years have been unusual and different, so we then took the same model and applied it to the previous 20 years—and got substantially identical results. This strongly supports the strength of the model.

Even if you look at the differences, they fall within acceptable and expected parameters. The higher drawdown in the 30-year data, for example, comes from the sudden market correction in 1987, which we have already discussed as a historically worst-case scenario.

Now for the next step. While averages can be useful, what matters are the year-to-year returns and, even more important, the multiyear returns. Let's look at how these ETF and index models behaved over multiyear periods during the past 30 years.

	1-year periods	3-year periods	5-year periods	10-year periods
Minimum	−9.34%	1.23%	1.75%	6.10%
Maximum	30.09%	19.51%	17.54%	12.43%
Average	9.62%	9.97%	9.91%	9.43%
Standard Deviation	7.91%	3.81%	2.93%	1.35%

These numbers were calculated by looking at all of the holding periods—12, 36, 60, and 120 months—in the 30-year period. There is considerable overlap, of course, but since an investor could start in any month, this covers all possibilities.

What you can see is that average returns for all periods ranged between 9 percent and 10 percent, with longer periods of five to ten years averaging around 9.5 percent to 9.9 percent. This looks, on the face of it, as though you can reasonably expect to get that 9.5 percent or so consistently, and we have met our goals. Hooray! But must we still worry about the risk of slow failure—of getting returns too low to meet our goals?

Failure from low minimum returns

Averages can be misleading. That is exactly why I have included minimum and maximum returns in the data. I am not worried about the maximums, as we can all figure out ways to spend the extra money, but minimums are a serious problem. Over time, if a minimum return is below the target return, you have slow failure no matter what the average is over a longer or shorter period.

Do we have this problem? Looking at the one-year results, they are quite consistent with the drawdown figures and with the return figures. On average, you would make just under 10 percent every year. Over the past 30 years, the worst you would have lost in any 12-month period was just under 10 percent.

It's at the multiyear time horizons, though, that the Main Street method really starts to shine. Over three- and five-year periods during the past 30 years, this method never lost money, while average returns ranged from 9 percent to 10 percent.

To understand the real advantage of the Main Street approach, let's compare the results with the same figures for a typical 60/40 buy-and-hold portfolio.

Seat Belt Portfolio

	1-year periods	3-year periods	5-year periods	10-year periods
Minimum	−9.34%	1.23%	1.75%	6.10%
Maximum	30.09%	19.51%	17.54%	12.43%
Average	9.62%	9.97%	9.91%	9.43%
Standard Deviation	7.91%	3.81%	2.93%	1.35%

60/40 Buy-and-Hold Portfolio

	1-year periods	3-year periods	5-year periods	10-year periods
Minimum	−27.65%	−7.24%	−2.26%	0.42%
Maximum	34.50%	26.53%	20.09%	15.34%
Average	10.69%	9.77%	9.28%	9.31%
Standard Deviation	11.22%	7.10%	5.55%	4.08%

Just as we did with the Seat Belt Portfolio, we can look at all of the holding periods—12, 36, 60, and 120 months—in that 30-year period. What we see is that average returns for all periods were quite close to those of the Main Street approach, between 9 percent and 11 percent, with longer periods of five to ten years averaging around 9.3 percent. This looks, on the face of it, as though we can reasonably expect to get that 9 percent or so consistently. Where is the Main Street advantage? It shows up in the minimum returns.

The one-year drawdown for the buy-and-hold portfolio—more than 27 percent, versus less than 10 percent for the Seat Belt Portfolio—is an obvious problem. This would potentially cripple a retirement plan. Less obviously, but even worse, is the 7-percent loss over three years, where the Seat Belt Portfolio had a small gain. With a 7-percent required return from inflation and withdrawals, this equates to a 42-percent loss (7-percent loss + 7-percent required gain x 3 years) in purchasing power over three years, which would hurt a retiree even more.

Taking it to the limit of the data presented, a 10-year annual rate of return of just over zero for a buy-and-hold portfolio, given our 7-percent return requirement, would lead to a 70-percent loss in purchasing power over that time frame, which would certainly guarantee failure in any investing journey. Compare this with the Seat Belt Portfolio, where the worst 10-year results equated to a 6-percent gain, which would at least get you very close to your goal. That difference is exactly the point of the Main Street approach and the Seat Belt Portfolio.

Crash test your portfolio

Let's sum up. On an average basis over the past 30 years, a typical retiree with a required 7-percent return might have done just fine with a 60/40 portfolio. Depending on the starting point during that time frame, however, that same retiree could have seen his or her portfolio crippled and his or her financial plans derailed.

Both slow and fast failure are entirely possible in a buy-and-hold portfolio, and they have occurred during the past 30 years, a time when the market has risen dramatically. The point of the Main Street approach is to eliminate as much of the downside risk as possible while maintaining return levels that allow investors to meet their goals. The numbers for the Seat Belt Portfolio show we have done that.

Earlier, we talked about the minimum return levels needed to meet some common goals. For college planning, we estimated this at around 6 percent; for retirement planning, the target is around 7 percent. Given these minimums, the figures above show that over any given five-year period over the past 30 years, the Main Street methodology would have allowed you to achieve your goals most of the time. Over a 10-year period, the portfolio would have worked virtually all the time.

Unfortunately, there are no guarantees. In the world of finance, *guarantee* is, quite literally, a forbidden word. You certainly won't see it here, any more than you will see it on a seat belt warranty that says you will never be hurt or killed in a car accident. We just can't offer that kind of reassurance.

I make these two points to underline something we will talk about in the next section. This method is not flawless. There are no guarantees, and this approach has a number of drawbacks that anyone considering it needs to accept.

On the other hand, based on history, this approach does have a very high probability of success over five years and an even greater probability over ten. This is as good as it gets on Wall Street *and* on Main Street. Remember, too, that these results represent the worst case. Making a small positive return is infinitely better than losing 10 percent, 20 percent, or even 30 percent.

What I've tried to do here is design a program directly aimed at Main Street. It does that. Now let's look at the drawbacks and costs.

DRAWBACKS AND COSTS

One of the problems with financial models is that you can assume away a lot of things. To this point, we have been discussing gross numbers. But there are many things that can affect the actual net returns. Transaction costs, for example. It costs money to trade stocks or ETFs, so you must account for the commissions. Taxes on any gains are another big example of what we wish we could assume away but can't in the real world. Finally, there's *fallibility*—no method works all the time. Let's look at all of these in the context of the Seat Belt Portfolio and see what they might mean going forward.

Taxes

By far, the biggest weakness of the Seat Belt investing model is its tax inefficiency. Buying and selling stocks or ETFs on a regular basis could result in substantial tax liability. You can minimize that tax liability by holding on to an investment vehicle for more than a year, but Uncle Sam will still get you. If you hold your investment for less than one year, you will be hit with taxes on your gains at the same rate as taxes on your ordinary income.

This is an unavoidable fact for taxable accounts. Many investors, however, have the bulk of their savings in tax-deferred retirement accounts, such as IRAs, SEP IRAs, 401(k)s, or 403(b)s. Trading in these accounts is tax deferred—that is, you do not have to pay taxes until you withdraw funds from the account. Taxes in the interim are, therefore, a nonissue.

Some of these accounts may have other problems, however. 401(k)s and 403(b)s, for example, may have restrictions on the kinds of assets that can be held or how they can be traded. Typically, holdings may be limited to mutual funds, and the plan sponsor may impose restrictions on how often you can trade or rebalance your account. Your individual circumstances will influence whether it makes sense to implement this program.

For college savings, there are tax-advantaged programs such as 529 plans, which are organized on a state level and offer similar tax advantages and operational restrictions as 401(k)s. For these and the restricted retirement accounts, a financial advisor may be able to help by making sure you are both aware of the opportunities and comply with the requirements.

So, there are ways around the tax problems with this approach, but the tax liability is definitely something to consider. This is not a unique issue; most investment products and strategies have tax burdens associated with them. Many mutual funds, for example, generate tax bills to investors because of their trading during the year. With our strategy, assets are, in many cases, owned for a year or more, which should minimize the tax bite.

Overall, when comparing the tax burden against the potential risk of loss, paying additional taxes may be a relatively minor issue for most investors. That is, however, a decision you should make consciously.

Transaction costs

We should consider two categories of costs. First are rebalancing costs, which are fees you pay when you buy and sell to get back to the prescribed mix of assets. As different parts of the portfolio gain and lose separately, the original balance will change over time. For example, stocks in a good year will rise much more than bonds, so at the end of the year you will own more stock than you want—and fewer bonds. Given that, you might have to sell some of the stock and buy some bonds to get back to your target allocation. In a bad year for stocks, of course, the reverse might be true.

Given the transaction mix from moving in and out of assets, rebalancing costs, for the most part, have not historically been a concern for the Seat Belt Portfolio, but they are still worth considering. Ways to deal with these costs include rebalancing on a quarterly rather than a monthly basis to reduce the number of transactions, waiting to rebalance until portfolio weights are substantially different from what they should be, or simply not rebalancing at all until a holding is sold.

For the buy and sell transactions based on market signals, when an asset class moves above or below its moving average, transaction costs should not be an issue either, as even for a relatively small portfolio, the potential loss associated with skipping a sell signal, or the foregone gain from skipping a buy signal, dwarfs the cost of the commission.

There are many discount brokers out there, and transaction costs are nowhere near what they used to be. Still, given regular trading, the costs for smaller portfolios can add up, so they need to be scrutinized. In any event, we will discuss this in the final section.

Fallibility

The final drawback I want to talk about is the fallibility of the model. If you remember, one of the first questions I asked at the start of the book was how can this approach blow up? More to the point, under what conditions will the Main Street approach fail to meet expectations?

Let's go back to our initial analysis of how we might fail—fast and slow—paying particular attention to when the portfolio, or parts of it, didn't work. Looking at 30 years of data should give us the real-world information to develop an understanding of how it might fail in the future.

Fast failure. Let's look at the monthly returns for the Seat Belt Portfolio. We do not need to look at all of them; the 10 worst monthly returns over the past 30 years are enough.

Month	Return
10/30/87	−9.76%
8/31/98	−6.42%
12/30/11	−5.61%
8/31/90	−5.19%
9/30/11	−4.97%
3/30/90	−4.77%
4/30/04	−4.16%
8/29/08	−4.16%
4/30/08	−3.45%
8/29/97	−3.23%

Looking at these numbers, there are a few surprises. October 1987, the largest one-day decline in stock market history, is not a surprise. Nor is August 1998, with the collapse of Long-Term Capital Management, a hedge fund that briefly threatened a crisis as bad as 2008. Nor, for that matter, are the April and August 2008 results a surprise. This was quite a bad year, but those were the two worst months.

These examples represent major systemic crises—and I would argue that they provide a good indicator of worst-case results. These are black months in Wall Street history, yet the results from the Seat Belt Portfolio—while not what we would like to see—still fall within our risk guidelines.

What is surprising are some of the other months included here—in particular, two months in 2011. It was a difficult year, but it was nowhere near as bad as the others, so what went wrong?

We can dig a little deeper to look at the returns of our portfolio components in each of these months, as outlined in the next chart.

	SPY	GLD	AGG	Return
10/30/87	−21.54%	2.02%	0.00%	−9.76%
8/31/98	−14.46%	0.00%	1.63%	−6.42%
12/30/11	0.00%	−12.31%	1.10%	−5.61%
8/31/90	−9.04%	0.00%	−1.34%	−5.19%
9/30/11	0.00%	−10.67%	0.73%	−4.97%
3/30/90	0.00%	−9.61%	0.07%	−4.77%
4/30/04	−1.57%	−8.31%	−2.60%	−4.16%
8/29/08	0.00%	−9.26%	0.95%	−4.16%
4/30/08	0.00%	−6.70%	−0.21%	−3.45%
8/29/97	−5.60%	0.00%	−0.85%	−3.23%

In the two worst months, in 1987 and 1998, the stock market was the culprit, with the S&P 500 down more than 20 percent in October 1987 and down almost 15 percent in August 1998. So, the reason for our portfolio losses is obvious. The same applies for August 1990. In 2011, on the other hand, the culprit was gold. Just as stocks can, gold has the potential to decline substantially in a one-month period. Gold dropped more than 10 percent in both September and December 2011. Clearly, it was a bad year for gold. Bonds, on the other hand, were never the cause of one of the 10 worst months.

What does this tell us? That volatile asset classes can result in short-term losses? We know that. That allocating a significant part of your portfolio to a volatile asset can result in losses? We know that, too. Is this problem avoidable?

Using the vocabulary we developed earlier, we can look at these results as an example of drawdown risk (i.e., fast failure). The results are not nearly as bad as the results experienced by other similar portfolios, such as the Wall Street 60/40 portfolio; nonetheless, they are enough to be uncomfortable. No one wants to lose 10 percent of his or her portfolio in a month. That hurts, and it's scary.

The reason I highlight these results is because we cannot avoid some level of risk in investing. We need to take risk—managed risk, well-understood risk, risk that we can't avoid. We simply must accept it, just as, frankly, we must accept the risk of an accident every time we get behind the wheel of a car.

What about the other form of risk—the slow failure of returns that do not meet our goals?

Slow failure. We talked about this a little bit earlier in the context of multiyear returns, and we saw that over one-, three-, and even five-year periods, there will be times when we won't meet our goals, and we must be prepared to accept that.

A subtler form of slow failure is underperformance with respect to the market. I call this the *brother-in-law effect,* and what I mean by it is that everyone has a brother-in-law—not mine, he's a great guy, but in theory—who brags about the money he made in the market or what a great stock he just picked. Somehow, he never seems to talk about the losers, just the winners.

It can be frustrating to watch the market run up and not participate in those gains. No less an authority than Warren Buffett noted that he had the same problem in the late 1990s and again in the mid-2000s. It is natural and inevitable that your portfolio will trail when the market is rising and you have less money in stocks than someone else. The Seat Belt Portfolio is very likely to underperform when the market is rising fast, for just this reason.

To see how this plays out, let's look at the annual returns of the Seat Belt Portfolio since 2009, when the stock market started rising, and compare them first with the S&P 500 and then with the Wall Street standard 60/40 portfolio. Remember, we have already seen these comparisons over the past 10 years, where our portfolio did well, but let's look at just the period after the crisis instead.

The years since 2009 have been a great time for the stock market, and we have seen markets go nowhere but up. How does our portfolio hold up against the S&P 500 in this period?

Looking at the dark line in comparison with the light line, we can see that the S&P 500, as represented by SPY, beat the pants off our portfolio. Arguably, that shouldn't be a surprise, as we hold other investments besides stocks, but you might be surprised at how many people compare a diversified portfolio like ours against the stock market itself.

Even if we compare our portfolio with Wall Street's standard 60/40, as represented by VBINX, per the chart on page 78, we still have been beaten. The two were running neck and neck until the start of 2012, when markets really took off.

Total Return (including all dividends): Dec. 31, 2008–Jun. 17, 2016

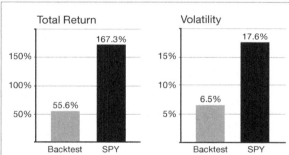

Total Return

Backtest: 55.6%
SPY: 167.3%

Volatility

Backtest: 6.5%
SPY: 17.6%

Summary Statistics

	CAGR	Max Drawdown		
Backtest	+6.1%	−6.4%	**Trades**	62
SPY	+14.1%	−27.1%	**Total Periods**	90
			Total Days	1,878

Winning periods	57	(63.8%)	**Losing periods**	33	(36.7%)
Periods outperformed benchmark	35	(38.9%)	**Periods underperformed benchmark**	55	(61.1%)
Best period		+6.74%	**Worst period**		−3.46%
Median winning period		+1.20%	**Median losing period**		−1.06%

Source: www.ETFreplay.com

Total Return (including all dividends): Dec. 31, 2008–Jun. 17, 2016

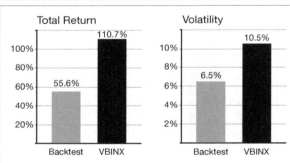

Total Return

- Backtest: 55.6%
- VBINX: 110.7%

Volatility

- Backtest: 6.5%
- VBINX: 10.5%

Summary Statistics

	CAGR	Max Drawdown
Backtest	+6.1%	−6.4%
VBINX	+10.5%	−17.5%

Trades	62
Total Periods	90
Total Days	1,878

Winning periods	57	(63.8%)	Losing periods	33	(36.7%)
Periods outperformed benchmark	39	(43.3%)	Periods underperformed benchmark	55	(56.7%)
Best period		+6.74%	Worst period		−3.46%
Median winning period		+1.20%	Median losing period		−1.06%

Source: www.ETFreplay.com

Since 2009, the 60/40 portfolio returns would have outpaced the Seat Belt Portfolio returns by almost half. We still preserved our edge in risk control, however, as the 60/40 portfolio was down more than 17 percent at one point while the Seat Belt Portfolio had a maximum drawdown of just over 6 percent. On a risk-adjusted basis, our portfolio was still competitive, but it can be tough to remember that when the return levels are as different as they are here.

It gets worse. If you look at the annual performance, the Seat Belt Portfolio has underperformed in every year since 2011—and it underperformed by more than 8 percent per year in 2012, 2013, and 2014.

What does this mean? Should we be worried? Is the model still valid? These are all questions that anyone would ask after a stock market run like this one, and this is another risk with this portfolio. The periods when the Seat Belt Portfolio underperforms are the periods when markets are rising to unsustainable levels and risk levels are increasing. As we have discussed earlier in the book, market valuations are at a level that they have exceeded only in 1929 and 2000. Yet the market keeps going up. That makes the risk level rise as well, and the need for a strategy like the Seat Belt Portfolio just gets greater—especially for investors who want to avoid a potential substantial loss.

Let's go back to the driving analogy. When I was younger, it used to bother me when people zipped past me doing 80 when I was doing 55. (Seriously. Ahem.) As I got older, though, and realized the risks those people were taking, it bothered me less. Now, my focus is more on getting to my destination safely rather than going faster than anyone else. It still gets me, though, when someone zips by.

Unfortunately, this is a core characteristic of the Main Street strategy, and it's unavoidable. The value of this approach does not come from outperforming when the market is going up; in fact, the strategy is likely to underperform at those times. No, the value of this strategy lies in the potential outperformance if the market goes down.

We will be passed at times—usually when the market is rising—and that underperformance will make you, as an investor, feel antsy. This, too, is a risk we simply must accept. If you want to minimize your drawdowns over time while still maintaining a sufficiently high level of returns, *you must accept that you may well underperform on the upside* even as you hope to outperform on the downside.

Comparing Main Street with Wall Street

As the final piece of the puzzle, let's compare the Seat Belt Portfolio against the most similar Wall Street strategy, the Permanent Portfolio mutual fund. If we can do better by buying and holding a mutual fund, we should do that. But can we?

Let's start with the Seat Belt Portfolio versus the Permanent Portfolio. As you know, the Permanent Portfolio is a good strategy, incorporating many of the same ideas we are using, so if we can beat it, that's probably a good sign. Let's go to the chart on page 81.

As we can see, the Seat Belt Portfolio tracks the Permanent Portfolio fairly closely most of the time. This is no surprise; we are using a similar asset mix. It outperforms, however, in the financial crisis and more recently, as the Seat Belt Portfolio is designed to step back from asset classes in trouble. Being able to get out of the market in troubled times has added perceptible value over and above the diversification provided in the Permanent Portfolio Fund.

Looking at the stats, the Seat Belt Portfolio performed better than the Permanent Portfolio in return terms, and it did so with about one-third of the risk, as measured by drawdowns. The Permanent Portfolio, while a good program, doesn't match the results of the Seat Belt Portfolio on a risk-adjusted basis.

A true strategy for Main Street

In the end, the Seat Belt Portfolio is built around what I consider the minimum risks necessary today to generate the returns you, as a Main Street investor, need to get to your destination. Investing is not easy. Even with a set of rules to guide us, when we set out on the journey, we must expect that, at times, we will get lost, be passed by cars going faster than us, and run into bad weather and traffic. The analogy with which we started has tremendous explanatory power as we seek to find our way into a college education or a comfortable retirement.

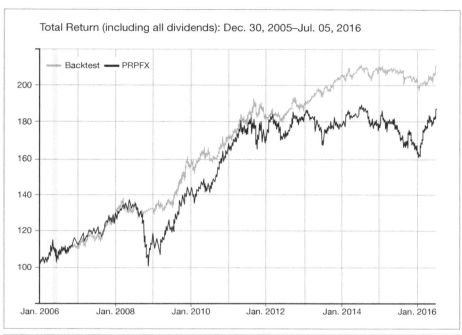

Total Return (including all dividends): Dec. 30, 2005–Jul. 05, 2016

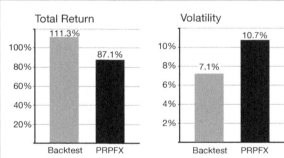

Total Return

Volatility

Summary Statistics

	CAGR	Max Drawdown
Backtest	+7.4%	−9.5%
PRPFX	+6.2%	−27.2%

Trades	79
Total Periods	127
Total Days	2,644

Winning periods	80	(63.0%)	Losing periods	47	(37.0%)
Periods outperformed benchmark	63	(49.6%)	Periods underperformed benchmark	64	(50.4%)
Best period		+6.74%	Worst period		−3.46%
Median winning period		+1.23%	Median losing period		−1.06%

Source: www.ETFreplay.com

Seat belts can save your life in a crash. When you're cruising along at 55 and somebody zips past doing 80, it is very tempting to put your foot on the gas—until, that is, you see that person 10 miles farther on having been pulled over by the police or, even worse, crashed by the side of the road. Then you'll be glad you stuck with 55, even if it seemed slow at the time.

Conditions will change. Markets will change. The economy will change. People, on the whole, will not. What makes the capital markets work is that investors can and do successfully complete journeys to a safe retirement or a funded college education. Especially here in the U.S., investors count on the markets being responsibly run and reasonably valued. By and large, that is what happens, but not always.

Main Street investing recognizes that the markets are not always rational and that stuff happens. We believe that when conditions get stormy, with rain coming down and the road starting to ice up, you need seat belts more than you need to go a bit faster. We would rather get there, perhaps a little bit later, but in one piece.

HOW TO START AND MANAGE
A SEAT BELT PORTFOLIO

We need to consider a couple of different scenarios when we talk about starting a Seat Belt Portfolio. First is starting from scratch with a taxable account or with a self-managed IRA or SEP. This is simple: pick a brokerage firm, deposit the money, and start trading. We will cover all those steps.

The second scenario is when you have an existing 401(k) or 403(b) plan or a 529 college savings plan. These plans are often run by third-party organizations, and, in many cases, they restrict your product selection, don't offer the ETFs we discussed, and limit how often you can trade those products. In these cases, you may need advice to figure out the best way to incorporate the Seat Belt Portfolio ideas into those wrappers. This is where a financial advisor may be helpful.

Opening a brokerage account
This is quite easy—look around. There are many good brokerage companies out there. The best one for you depends on your own individual needs and preferences.

Starting and running the Seat Belt Portfolio
Once we open a brokerage account and make our initial deposit, we need to do the following:

1. Determine what asset classes we want to include in our portfolio.
2. Determine whether those asset classes are above their moving averages or not.

3. Buy the ones that are.

4. Update regularly. I have used monthly updates throughout the book, but I've included a discussion of quarterly updates in this section as well.

Determining what asset classes to hold in the portfolio

Of the four asset classes—stocks, bonds, gold, and cash—stocks and bonds are mandatory, but you may want to consider whether to include gold and cash as well.

Gold, as we saw earlier, has led to several of the major monthly declines our portfolio experienced over time. It is a volatile and, as I write this, highly valued asset class. Although it led to improved returns over the past 10 and 30 years, much of that performance came in the 2000s, and it may not be repeated. Finally, gold, in many respects, is not an investment but instead a hedge against things going bad. You could very reasonably leave out gold and still get good results.

I do not recommend that, but I have included this discussion to address the people who are uncomfortable with gold as an investment. Using the GLD ETF instead of the physical metal has addressed many of the very real concerns associated with owning gold directly—theft, storage costs, transaction costs, and inconvenience—but for people who just do not like gold, it is okay to leave it out.

Cash can serve two roles in the Seat Belt Portfolio. As a placeholder for an asset class that is below its moving average, cash is unavoidable. As a separate asset class of its own, held as a buffer like in the Permanent Portfolio, it is not included in the portfolio, but it is something you may want to consider. Adding cash as a separate category not only reduces volatility even further, but it can make rebalancing easier. This reduction in the fast failure risk of drawdowns comes, of course, at the price of lower returns, raising the risk of slow failure. Overall, I do not recommend its inclusion, as the portfolio as designed meets our risk control goals, but if you are very risk averse, you might want to set aside some of your portfolio as cash and accept the likely lower returns.

The question for bonds is whether you want to leave them in the portfolio always or use the moving average strategy. As we noted earlier, over the past 10 years, using a moving average strategy resulted in inferior results. For a variety of reasons, I do not think that will necessarily be the case going forward, but it could be. A very defensible decision is to keep the bonds in the portfolio always and reconsider using moving averages every year or so.

What I'm recommending here, however, is that you use the moving average technique with bonds for two reasons: First, for consistency, so when you rebalance, or you apply the same technique to all asset classes; and second, because I believe interest rates are likely to rise over the next several years, and the moving average strategy will potentially provide some protection, even if it does not add much value in the short term.

Finally, the asset class of stocks is essential to the portfolio. Stocks provide the growth that we are counting on, and we need to use the moving average technique to manage their volatility. It won't always be successful, of course, but it's something that will provide us with much of the security we need.

The rest of this section will assume that we include stocks, bonds, and gold as the primary asset classes, with cash as a placeholder.

Determining whether the asset classes are above their moving averages

For each of the asset classes, we must determine where they are with respect to the moving average. We will use a 10-month, or 200-day, moving average in this analysis—and check it every time we rebalance. In this case, we are using trading days (i.e., days the stock market is open).

The easiest way to check where the asset classes are is to go to
Yahoo Finance: *finance.yahoo.com.*

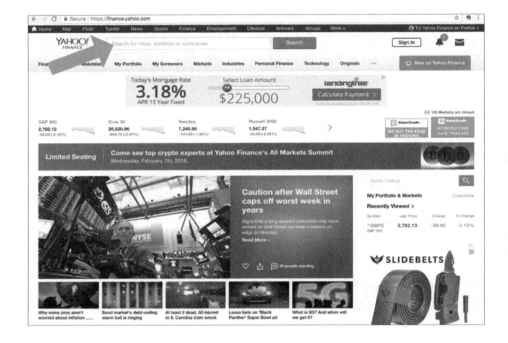

Next, click in the Quote Lookup box and type the ETF you want to research.
In this case, we'll use SPY, which will take us to a screen like the following.

From here, you must do two things. First, click on the Chart link at the top, as shown by the arrow.

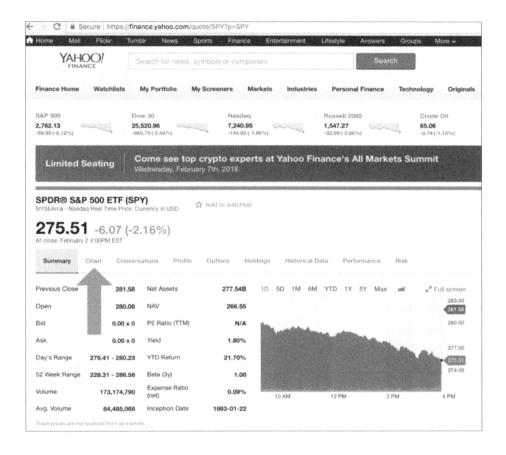

This will bring you to a page similar to the following. Click on Indicators, as shown by the arrow below, and select Moving Average from the list under Commonly Used. This will add moving averages to your screen.

In the next screen that appears, replace 50 with 200 and click Save. The 200-day moving average will display on your chart (here, it is the lower line in the image at the bottom of page 88).

You can see from the screenshot that, at the time I wrote this, the SPY ETF was well above its 200-day moving average (again, the bottom line). If we were setting up the portfolio today, we would be buying into SPY.

Be sure to follow this same process to review GLD and AGG; your results will look something like the images on page 90, depending on when you run your analysis. You can see that gold is above its 200-day moving average, so if we were starting the portfolio based on this information, we would include gold. AGG is below its 200-day moving average, so we would *not* include AGG in the portfolio.

Buying the asset classes

Once we determine which asset classes we are going to include in any given month, we then need to determine how we are going to spread out our investments. In this case, we would buy only two: stocks and gold. Should we allocate 50 percent to each if we buy only two, because, at this point, bonds are below their 200-day moving average? Or will we allocate 33 percent to each of our three asset classes, using cash instead of bonds?

The trade-off is that allocating more to an asset class gives you more exposure to the risk of a decline in that asset class. In this case, for example, we would allocate 50 percent to stocks if we decided to split the actual investment evenly among included assets. This is not necessarily a problem—you'll remember that the Wall Street balanced portfolio typically held 60 percent in stocks—but it does dial up the risk, relatively speaking. It also, at least over the past couple of decades, would dial up the return. It really is a trade-off.

What I'm recommending, and what the historical data set test was based on, is a maximum 33-percent allocation for any asset class *except* cash. In other words, even if stocks or gold or bonds were the only asset class above the 200-day moving average and thus the only asset class included in the portfolio, only one-third of your money would be invested; the rest would stay in cash. If you think about it, if two of the three asset classes are both that weak, things are getting worrying, and a strong cash position makes sense.

In this case, with both stocks and gold above the 200-day moving average, they would be included in the portfolio at one-third weight: 33 percent for stocks and 33 percent for gold, with the remainder in cash. (Remember, we're excluding bonds, as they are below the moving average line.) So, if we had a $60,000 portfolio, we would look to invest $20,000 into the SPY ETF and $20,000 into the GLD ETF, leaving $20,000 in cash.

Having made those purchases, we would sit back and wait until the next rebalancing date, and then repeat the process.

How often should you update your Seat Belt Portfolio?

Rebalancing decisions are based around costs. Depending on your cost to trade, you will be spending about $15 per rebalance. For a medium-size Seat Belt Portfolio, say $50,000, if you rebalanced every month, at an average cost of about $15, that would cost you about one-third of a percent per year, which I consider reasonable given the relative performance advantage of monthly rebalances.

On the other hand, with a smaller portfolio of, say, $10,000, that cost would be more than 2 percent of your portfolio, which is probably too much. In this case, you might want to rebalance quarterly, with the intention of increasing the frequency as the portfolio grows. Equally, you might feel that the improved risk and return of a monthly update is worth the extra cost.

Throughout this book, I've looked at monthly portfolio updates. I tested several different periods, and monthly seemed to be optimal for most portfolio sizes in the Main Street universe. As a comparative exercise, though, and for the benefit of those with smaller portfolios, let's look at the results of monthly (page 93) versus quarterly (page 94) rebalancing since 2005.

As you can see, quarterly rebalancing results in lower returns with somewhat higher risk. The difference is not severe—the Main Street investing approach still works—but it equates to an additional 7-percent gain for the portfolio updated monthly since 2005.

If you want to try to quantify this, the additional transaction costs of about $120 make sense when the portfolio is around $25,000 and you want to keep annual transaction costs below 0.50 percent, which is a reasonable goal. For portfolios below that amount, quarterly rebalancing might make more sense.

An example of a portfolio update

As an example of what we have been talking about, let's walk through what a typical update would look like. Let's assume we hold all three asset classes in our portfolio—SPY, GLD, and AGG—and then we learn that AGG has dropped below the moving average. For the next month, we want to own SPY and GLD, but not AGG.

Total Return (including all dividends): Dec. 31, 2004–Jun. 17, 2016

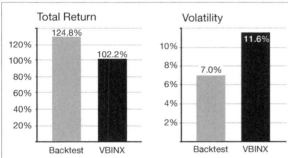

Total Return

Volatility

Summary Statistics

	CAGR	Max Drawdown
Backtest	+7.3%	−9.5%
VBINX	+6.3%	−36.0%

Trades	85
Total Periods	138
Total Days	2,885

Winning periods	88	(63.8%)	Losing periods	47	(36.2%)
Periods outperformed benchmark	66	(47.8%)	Periods underperformed benchmark	64	(52.2%)
Best period		+6.74%	Worst period		−3.46%
Median winning period		+1.23%	Median losing period		−1.05%

Total Return (including all dividends): Dec. 31, 2004–Jun. 17, 2016

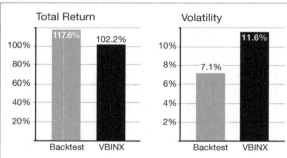

Total Return

Volatility

Summary Statistics

	CAGR	Max Drawdown
Backtest	+7.0%	−10.0%
VBINX	+6.3%	−36.0%

Trades	56
Total Periods	46
Total Days	2,885

Winning periods	34	(73.9%)	Losing periods	12	(26.1%)
Periods outperformed benchmark	20	(43.5%)	Periods underperformed benchmark	26	(56.5%)
Best period		+9.17%	Worst period		−2.61%
Median winning period		+2.26%	Median losing period		−0.70%

To make things easy, let's assume we have $60,000 in the portfolio divided evenly among all three. Our holdings are as follows:

Asset	Current	Target	Change
SPY	1/3 – $20,000	1/3 – $20,000	None
GLD	1/3 – $20,000	1/3 – $20,000	None
AGG	1/3 – $20,000	0/3 – $0	Sell $20,000
Cash	0/3 – $0	1/3 – $20,000	+$20,000

There is one transaction here, for a cost of, say, $8–$12, which should be typical for a month with transactions. If we were adding AGG or any of the other holdings back in, there would be the same number of transactions, but reversed, and the same costs. Note also that, for many months, there will be no transactions at all.

To give you some idea of how often you might need to modify your portfolio, let's look at each asset class in our Seat Belt Portfolio individually and then at the portfolio as a whole for the time frame from 2005 through June 2016, a period of 138 months. Here's how many transactions would have occurred:

- **Stocks:** Six moves in and out for a total of 12 transactions
- **Bonds:** Seven moves in and out for a total of 14 transactions
- **Gold:** Eight moves in and out for a total of 16 transactions
- **Total portfolio:** 38 months with allocation changes

Note that the number of months our total portfolio required changes is less than the total number of transactions. That's because, in some months, there were changes in more than one asset class.

On average, there will be four transactions per year, and, overall, about one out of every four months will require a portfolio update. This would equate to average trading costs of around $100 per year, although this is misleading because the transactions tend to be clustered as markets go through turbulence. Nonetheless, from a planning perspective, it's useful to look at average costs, as higher costs in one year will be offset by lower costs in other years.

For a specific example, let's look at the last major market drawdown, in 2008–2009. The stock portion of the portfolio went to cash in December 2007, while gold went to cash in August 2008, and bonds went to cash in October 2008. Note that as the crisis deepened, the portfolio allocations automatically de-risked. In January 2009, with the storm fading, we would have bought back into bonds and gold; the allocation to stocks would have been added back in July 2009. By using these signals, and reallocating, your portfolio would have ridden out the crisis and been well positioned to participate in the rebound.

A quick summary

We have covered a great deal in the past chapter, so let's look back to make sure we understand.

When to update. Monthly or perhaps quarterly. In either case, values may bounce around above and below the moving average during the time period, but we only update on the appropriate day. If that is the first weekday of the month, for example, and the markets decline on the tenth, we wait until the first day of the following month. This helps us to avoid being whipsawed as markets bounce around and ensures that we react only to larger moves in the market.

What to do. The following chart summarizes what your holdings would be when you update, depending on the signals from each of the asset classes.

Signals	Holdings
SPY – above 200-day average GLD – above AGG – above	SPY – 33% GLD – 33% AGG – 33% Cash – 1%
SPY – above 200-day average GLD – below AGG – above	SPY – 33% GLD – 0% AGG – 33% Cash – 34%
SPY – above 200-day average GLD – above AGG – below	SPY – 33% GLD – 33% AGG – 0% Cash – 34%
SPY – below 200-day average GLD – above AGG – above	SPY – 0% GLD – 33% AGG – 33% Cash – 34%
SPY – above 200-day average GLD – below AGG – below	SPY – 33% GLD – 0% AGG – 0% Cash – 67%
SPY – below 200-day average GLD – below AGG – above	SPY – 0% GLD – 0% AGG – 33% Cash – 67%
SPY – below 200-day average GLD – above AGG – below	SPY – 0% GLD – 33% AGG – 0% Cash – 67%
SPY – below 200-day average GLD – below AGG – below	SPY – 0% GLD – 0% AGG – 0% Cash – 100%

NEXT STEPS

This takes us to where we set out to go. We now have a solid investment portfolio, designed to get us to our destination as quickly as possible while minimizing the chances of a life-threatening crash. Well done! This is a major step toward achieving your financial goals.

Are you done? Not necessarily. This book focuses on investing, which is both necessary and important, but there are many other areas of your financial life you need to review—insurance, tax planning, and how to best claim and manage social security benefits, to name a few. This book will, however, help you build the foundation on which everything else must rest.

As you think about the next step, allow me to recommend professional assistance. Financial advisors can provide real value in the areas I discuss here and others. I know a lot about investing, but not nearly as much about financial planning, so I work with an advisor myself. A good financial advisor can make your life easier and more financially secure while helping you pursue the goals important to you and/or your family. I am privileged to work with some of the best in the business, and I certainly value what they do.

The Seat Belt Portfolio is a great foundation for your investments, but there are certainly ways to extend and improve it. For example, I personally use this methodology, but I apply it to a wider range of asset classes than are used in the book. More immediately, financial advisors might be able to help you manage your portfolio or provide ideas on how to expand it to help you meet your goals. Keep the foundation, but don't be afraid to add other investments that can potentially improve your outcome.

If you think about it, just as we designed our portfolio to get us to our destination with a minimum amount of risk, there are many other tools out there that can help us do the same for the rest of our lives. It only makes sense to try to find them. For me, a financial advisor has been invaluable in doing just that.

IN CONCLUSION

If you've read this far, thank you. I wrote this book to give the average investor—the Main Street investor—a different way to think about investing. The industry provides a great deal of useful information and strategies, but it does not necessarily make that information easy to use. I hope I have shed some light on a different way to use the many resources out there.

I also wanted to demonstrate some ways to take control of your own financial journey. Like driving a car, there are things about investing that you must know, hazards you must worry about, and things that are worth paying attention to. Like anyone who enjoys the freedom of using a car to get to where he or she wants to go, investors will find freedom in being able to direct their investments using a strategy that has shown itself to be equally as effective at getting them to their destination. Yes, there are risks, but you now have a better idea of what they are—and how to add seat belts to help you mitigate them.

If you take nothing else away from the book, I hope you realize that you can succeed as an investor. It does not have to be that hard, and we have tools available today that make it easier than ever.

You can meet your financial goals over time.

You do not have to take as much risk as you think.

You can do it.

ACKNOWLEDGMENTS

I owe an enormous debt of gratitude to the staff and advisors of Commonwealth Financial Network. I have learned so much from working with them, and have benefited so much from my time there, that it is impossible to quantify. I am privileged to associate with so many fine people. Thank you, all.

Of those who read and commented on earlier versions of this book, I can certainly single out Wayne Bloom for his exceptionally helpful insight. This is a much better book for your candid feedback, and I am very grateful for your time and support.

Other readers who gave their time and valuable comments include Paul Tolley, Brian Price, and Joe Tully from Commonwealth; my friends Paul Cantor, Brad Phillips, Richard Band, and Todd Estabrook; and, last but not least, my parents, Bill and Katie. I should also mention the many people here at Commonwealth with whom I have discussed the concepts behind this book and who all contributed their thoughts as well.

The move from manuscript to book is a much longer journey than I initially thought—much like investing—and it would not have happened without the hard work of Kate Flood, who, as usual, did wonderful editorial work, and Christina Terry, the graphic designer who made the following pages much easier on the eye. Thank you, both—the book would not exist without you.

Again, my gratitude to all of you knows no bounds.

Any remaining errors are, of course, all mine.